A CENTURY of
DONCASTER

An old Doncaster Corporation bus (no. 94) is driven past the Mansion House to celebrate the centenary of public transport in Doncaster, Sunday 2 June 2002. The cavalcade followed part of the course of the first tram journey of 1902 and proceeded to Hexthorpe Flatts for the main rally. *(Author)*

A CENTURY *of* DONCASTER

BRIAN ELLIOTT

WILLIAM COTTERILL CLARK. MAYOR. 1873.

First published in the United Kingdom in 2002 by
Sutton Publishing Limited exclusively for
WHSmith, Greenbridge Road, Swindon SN3 3LD

British Library Cataloguing in Publication Data
A catalogue record for this book is available from the British Library.

ISBN 0-7509-3145-0

Illustrations

Front endpaper: A wonderful early view of part of the old market place, *c.* 1903. In particular, note the prominence of W.E. Cox, who dealt in fruit and potatoes as well as fish. The traditional baskets, wooden barrels and boxes are typical features. Most of the traders remain still and face the intrepid photographer. The man standing on the dray and the boys in the foreground attract the eye in a really superb composition. There is also a good view of the Market Inn, where Alfred Braithwaite was publican, and F.W. Fisher's shop, both under a pleasing Georgian façade. The building of the Market Hall (1846) and Corn Exchange (1873) alongside the Wool and Cattle Markets coincided with Doncaster's emergence as a railway centre of national importance. It also confirmed its position as one of the premier market towns in the north of England. *(Author's Collection)*
Back endpaper: Doncaster's changing townscape can be appreciated in this modern aerial photograph. St George's Church stands out, especially after the recent improvements to the access roads and urban environment to the south and east of this magnificent building. The new St George's roundabout and bridge are also distinctive and spectacular features. We also have a good view of the 'brown field' area to the north-west of the town centre, scheduled for extensive development within the context of the Doncaster Renaissance Town Charter 2002. *(DMBC)*
Half title page: Members of the Doncaster Amateur Operatic Group in period costume outside the Mansion House, 16 June 2002. They were promoting a forthcoming music hall performance as well as being a most welcome attraction for the Centenary Transport Rally, shortly to pass by. *(Author)*
Title page: Attractive and interesting detail rewards anyone who cares to look above the main entrance to the Corn Exchange. The old Guild Hall and Mansion House are depicted on either side of the sculpted figures. The architect was William Watkins of Lincoln. *(Author)*

Typeset in 11/14pt Photina and produced by
Sutton Publishing Limited, Phoenix Mill,
Thrupp, Stroud, Gloucestershire GL5 2BU.
Printed and bound in England by
J.H. Haynes & Co. Ltd, Sparkford.

Contents

The Mansion House, June 2002. It was back in 1738 that the corporation decided to begin the process of obtaining land on a suitable site for the creation of a municipal building, perhaps inspired by the only other Yorkshire example, at York. In 1744 James Paine, a young architect already working for Sir Rowland Winn at Nostell Priory, was appointed to undertake the design, though interestingly the original façade is a copy of Inigo Jones's seventeenth-century design for the royal palace of Whitehall. (Information courtesy of Brian Barber.) Paine's estimate for the cost of building was a little over £4,523 but that did not include the considerable expense of internal features and furnishings. Doncaster's Mansion House was officially opened on 15 April 1749. In 1801 the upper part of the building was transformed and a new storey added by the noted local architect William Lindley. A banqueting hall was completed five years later. Another local man, William Hurst, was responsible for the extensive alterations of 1831. *(Author)*

DONCASTER
Doncaster Metropolitan Borough Council

Foreword

The Borough of Doncaster is rightly proud of its key role in driving the economic development of our nation from the Industrial Revolution through both the nineteenth and twentieth centuries. Two particular industries stand out. First, we produced the coal that fed the powerhouse of our country's prosperity. We also became famous for technological advances in the railway industry, producing over 2,500 locomotives from the Plant Works, including the world-famous *Flying Scotsman* and *Mallard*, the latter being the fastest steam train ever built. Doncaster also has a worldwide

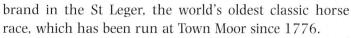

brand in the St Leger, the world's oldest classic horse race, which has been run at Town Moor since 1776.

Today, we face many new economic and social challenges as we build a new economy in Doncaster, and although the old industries have largely gone new ones based on logistics and hi-tech manufacturing are beginning to emerge.

A Century of Doncaster not only presents us with the opportunity to reflect on the rich history and heritage that our forebears have left us but also allows us to celebrate our modern achievements. It gives us confidence to remember that Doncaster is a special town and we must redouble our efforts to ensure that its future is every bit as exciting and noteworthy as its past.

Martin Winter
Mayor of Doncaster

Stanley Frith, aged ninety-two, being presented with a framed memento in recognition of his long service to public transport, by Doncaster's civic mayor, Councillor John Quinn. The occasion took place at Hexthorpe Flatts during the Centenary Transport Rally, on Sunday 2 June 2002. Stanley worked as a teenage tram conductor in the early 1930s, the twilight era of the trams. He progressed to drive trolley- and motor-buses and was the town's senior driver; he drove Doncaster's last trolleybus in 1963. Stanley has many anecdotes about his early working life, including the first time he worked on his own as a conductor, completing a marathon thirteen-hour stint on the Hyde Park route. At the end of the day, and much to the amusement of the passengers, young Stanley had accumulated over £4 in coppers (about a thousand coins) and could hardly carry his leather money bag. He had not realised that it was the custom for conductors to change their cash at pubs where grateful licensees would give out five Players Weights cigarettes 'for ten bob's worth' of change! *(Author)*

Introduction

Although the *Doncaster Chronicle* reported on 30 May 1902 that 'all manner of accidents are being predicted for Doncaster's new plaything', hundreds of people queued for a tram ride when the new system opened on Monday 2 June. Pinafores were presented to about 700 women with children who purchased tickets to ride on the day. The first day's takings amounted to £43 19*s* 5*d* for an estimated 10,553 paying passengers but hundreds gained free rides, the hard-pressed conductors being unable to cope. The *Chronicle*, however, 'congratulated the Corporation . . . on the class of car they have adopted', which were 'handsome and thoroughly well-built coaches'. Each was described as 'capacious, well upholstered [with] an admirably fitted saloon . . . lighted in the daytime by six large plate-glass windows, three a side, and at night time by six electric lamps'. The seats were 'comfortable' and 'warmly rugged' and there were easily reached 'call-bells overhead'. We are also informed that the cars carried 56 passengers, 24 inside and 32 outside, 'the light seats on the roof adding but little to the total weight of the car'. A 'warm tone of maroon' was chosen for the body of the carriages, which were 'finely varnished . . . the Doncaster arms and motto being prettily emblazoned in the centre of both sides'. The 'upper parts and under carriage are finished in pale yellow', the latter bearing the inscription 'Doncaster Corporation Tramways'. The Doncaster tram service staggered on until June 1935 but vehicles had been gradually withdrawn from 1927, more or less coinciding with the introduction of trolleybuses. Then a new transport era began in the town. The Grand Centenary Transport Rally held at Hexthorpe Flatts on Sunday 2 June 2002 attracted a great deal of interest and included a 'ceremonial first tram journey' from the Mansion House – in reality a procession of public service vehicles, led by the civic car and a 1953 former Corporation bus.

Nowadays Doncaster is emerging from the doldrums of the 1980s and early 1990s when funding problems coincided with an understandable lack of confidence in some public officials. The award-winning Quality Streets Programme, completed in five phases over six years (1995–2001) with the help of external funding, has transformed the town centre, creating a much more pleasant urban environment for all. Public works of art, innovative street furniture, resurfacing and better lighting have all contributed to the success, as has the involvement of schoolchildren and local people in the planning and design process. The recent completion of the new St George's Bridge and the ongoing refurbishment of the old North Bridge, the proposed new transport interchange, plans for the development of the racecourse and for a community sports stadium, a revived market and Waterdale cultural area and long-term developments on Doncaster Lakeside should all form part of the regeneration of Doncaster. The launch of the *Doncaster Renaissance Town Charter 2002*, setting out how Doncaster could look over the next twenty-five years, carries on this forward-thinking and consultative approach.

Researching and writing *A Century of Doncaster* in a 'photohistory' format has been a tremendous challenge but also a great opportunity to look at an important town during a period of great change. Time pressures apart, my main concern was to gather together a sufficient number, range and quality of images in order to give some indication of the changing face of Doncaster and its people over a long time-scale. I refer to 'people' quite deliberately as I did not want the book to consist entirely of a chronology of street scenes and buildings. Chapters entitled People & Occasions, Entertainment & Employment and Sport for All should help to meet my aim of a more social approach. I have selected the images with a great deal of care and have tried to

Looking across to St George's Church from Friary Closes, *c.* 1905. A keel boat attached to a mooring post on the Sheffield & South Yorkshire Navigation adds interest to the scene. The church was then little more than fifty years old. The distinguished architect Sir Gilbert Scott was commissioned to design Doncaster's fine Victorian parish church, completed in 1854–8 and described by Pevsner as 'the most cathedral-like' of his churches. St George's replaced Doncaster's medieval parish church of St Mary's which had a famous crossing tower, a feature incorporated with panache in Scott's magnificent composition. The prolific Victorian was also busy at Doncaster Grammar School, Christ Church and St John's at Cadeby. *(Author's Collection)*

This photograph was taken from a similar viewpoint almost a hundred years later, on 16 June 2002. St George's is one of the best and most complete Victorian town churches in the north of England – and thanks to recent urban improvements by Doncaster Council it can now be appreciated from a number of aspects. Today's developing waterfront area certainly adds interest to the modern scene. *(Author)*

enhance their visual impact by the use of meaningful captions, although any errors are my own. The first two chapters are devoted to what I term 'Old Doncaster', covering much of the first half of the twentieth century (or what could reasonably be called the tram and trolleybus era). Here we can see a Doncaster far removed from modern times, before the large-scale changes to the town's appearance that began to take place during the 1960s. The latter was a time when Doncaster lost many interesting buildings and in the process a great deal of character, though it could be argued that the town fared better than some of its neighbours. I also feel there is much to celebrate and look forward to in our modern town, which explains my choice of New Doncaster as the title of my final chapter.

I moved to live in the Doncaster area from neighbouring Barnsley seventeen years ago, at about the time when great pits such as Brodsworth Main and Yorkshire Main were being obliterated from the local landscape with such undue haste. As a teenager in the

The Doncaster A1M bypass under construction. This view – by an amateur photographer – looks north from the Albert Bridge, Sprotbrough, and was taken on 4 June 1961. *(Cockayne/Alan Paley)*

early 1960s I travelled daily to Doncaster from Barnsley on a no. 14 Yorkshire Traction bus and then walked or caught another bus to alight near the racecourse as I was employed in those days as an apprentice professional footballer at Doncaster Rovers' Belle Vue ground. I got to know the older Doncaster quite well during the twilight of the trolleybus era. As a relative newcomer, but with some Doncaster connections, I hope my present interpretation will benefit from a degree of objectivity but I am also very grateful for the recent contributions of others towards the compilation of the book. My experience in working with a variety of local writers during the late 1990s, when I edited the two-volume *Aspects of Doncaster* books, certainly demonstrated to me that there was an enormous interest in local and family history in the area.

In a sense Bernard Cuttriss started the ball rolling with his regular features in the *Doncaster Gazette* on the theme of 'Old Doncaster', and the compilation of his 1963 book of the same title, from his own private picture library, was a landmark publication for a developing genre. Cuttriss was writing at a time when the townscape of Doncaster was beginning to undergo massive change; as happened in all the neighbouring towns, many interesting and historic buildings were demolished. His articles and his book served a nostalgic need to look back over sixty years but the images and captions meant that the book both appealed to and inspired later historians.

Compiling this book would have been impossible without the help, cooperation and encouragement of many people and organisations. For modern Doncaster, I could not have had better support from a variety of departments of Doncaster Metropolitan Council. As usual the staff at the Local Studies Library and the Reference Library have been very helpful and officers at Danum House and Scarbrough House were equally accommodating. I am grateful in particular to Neil Firth who provided excellent advice and guidance relating to the modern town centre.

What made the project so enjoyable was meeting so many people who were happy to share information and material during the course of my research visits and interviews. It was marvellous to travel to Hunmanby and meet retired police officer Alan Paley and his wife Valerie. Meeting 92-year-old former tram conductor and trolleybus driver Stanley Frith at the Doncaster Centenary Transport Rally in Hexthorpe Flatts was an unexpected bonus, as was a chat with Olympic archer and gold medallist Anita Chapman and her husband Bernie. Martin Sills, Secretary of Doncaster Belles Ladies Football Club, was kind enough to answer my request for information and material and Roger Tuby allowed me

The new St George's Bridge is a spectacular addition to Doncaster's developing townscape. The view from the waterfront area is a particularly attractive one. (*Author*)

access to his showman family archives. I am also very grateful to my friends Chris Sharp and Norman Ellis, who allowed me to select from their extensive collections of old postcards, and to local freelance photographer Eric Hepworth, who was happy for me to use some of his superb sporting images. Lastly, my thanks go to Simon Fletcher, Michelle Tilling, Sarah Moore and all at Sutton Publishing for their help and encouragement.

In May 2002 Doncaster became one of the first towns in the country to elect a mayor. In his speech at a press conference shortly after his victory, Martin Winter said: 'This is a step in putting the past behind us and making a fresh start.' I would like to thank Martin for writing the Foreword to this book and for supporting the project.

Brian Elliott
July 2002

Trolleybus driver Stanley Frith and his 'clippie', conductress 'Dot' Northern, at the Warmsworth/Balby terminus, Barrel Lane, in the 1950s. *(Stanley Frith)*

From Trams to Trolleybuses

The Station Road area of town was popular with Edwardian photographers. Here the crossroads with its tall and attractive buildings form a wonderful backdrop for the new trams. Station Road was planned as the terminus for all routes (except Bentley) so it was always a busy scene. This is one of the first postcards produced of the area. It was posted in 1903 and the message was limited to the small space at the lower front part of the card. The sender's comments reflect the novel means of travel: 'What do you think to our trams [?]. The first one I go home to tea in.' *(Author's Collection)*

This marvellous early photograph by Edward Leonard Scrivens features two of the most splendid late Victorian buildings on Station Road: the gleaming new Grand Theatre of 1899 and the 1880s William and Glyn Temperance Hotel, with its graceful rounded profile at the junction of Factory Lane. The driving force behind the Grand Theatre and Opera House was local entrepreneur John William Chapman, who ran a variety of agencies in Doncaster. He had bought the Empire Palace (Circus) Theatre which was demolished in early July 1898 to make way for the Grand, which opened on 27 March the following year, just two days after the last performance at Doncaster's old theatre built in 1776. John P. Briggs was consulting architect for the Grand and local firm Harold Arnold & Sons were the building contractors. The 'Glyn' was named after the Revd Edward Carr Glyn, Vicar of St George's and a founder member of the local temperance movement. *(Chris Sharp Collection/Old Barnsley)*

The full grandeur of Station Road could be captured if the photographer assembled his equipment at the end of Printing Office Street, as was the case in this splendid example, dating from about 1903. The Doncaster Mutual Cooperative Society Building of 1897 with its graceful electric lamps stands proudly opposite the Turkish Baths and the clock tower of the aptly named Oriental Buildings. Just discernible in the centre, behind the policeman, is what remains of the Stirling Monument. The no. 14 tram (part of the original 1902 consignment) is bound for Balby via Hexthorpe. *(Author's Collection)*

Carriages wait at Doncaster station on this postcard sent from Doncaster in November 1915. There was no platform or subway, and passengers had to walk across the line to reach the opposite Down platform. *(Norman Ellis Collection)*

Tram no. 24, with New Village on its indicator, appears to be standing at the Bentley New Village terminus. This was one of the original 'open-toppers' used by the corporation; a roof was added to the upper deck in about 1907–13. The front panel looks somewhat battered, so the vehicle may have been photographed towards the end of its working life around the late 1920s or early 1930s. The conductor Ron Adamson and the driver are smartly dressed as per regulation. Stanley Frith told me that he was occasionally reprimanded for heinous offences against these regulations, such as not wearing a cap! He also mentioned that the drivers had a terrible time of it in winter, having to stand for hours with no windscreen; in fact sometimes their hands and arms 'froze solid' – and all for less than £3 a week. (*Norman Ellis Collection*)

This is another interesting early Scrivens photograph, taken from Station Road looking towards St Sepulchre Street and the junction of Printing Office Street where a tram passes by. We have a good view of the impressive Benefit Boots & Shoes store (built in 1898), Ernest Water's drapery and millinery shop (with its first-floor 'Mourning Warehouse') and Taylor & Colbridge stationer's shop. On Station Road we can just see two other shopfronts: A.W. Bettles (watchmaker and jeweller) and Cornelius & Inchbold (outfitters and tailors). *(Chris Sharp Collection/Old Barnsley)*

The Benefit Boot & Shoe emporium can also be seen on this later (*c.* 1938) postcard showing a busy St Sepulchre Street. The Taylor & Colbridge stationer's shop also presents an impressive façade and a trolleybus can be seen progressing along the left side of the street. This side was to be lost in the mid-1960s during the development of the Arndale (Frenchgate Centre). The first 'trackies' or trackless buses appeared on the streets of Doncaster in 1928. *(Norman Ellis Collection)*

There is much splendid detail on the red-brick Benefit Boot & Shoe building, with its attractive features in sandstone. The clock is set between elegant carved figures and the Latin inscription *Omni Labor Vincit* ('Work conquers all things'). Virgil was describing the harshness of Roman life following the Golden Age when the earth 'yielded its fruits without labour' but his phrase provided a perfect motto for a late Victorian business that depended so much on working-class patronage in northern industrial towns. A similar building existed in neighbouring Sheffield. *(Author)*

Modern St Sepulchre Gate. The plain and stark vertical lines of the Frenchgate Centre contrast sharply with the interesting façades on the opposite side of the street, but the tower of St George's is difficult to appreciate from this viewpoint. The Council's Quality Streets project has provided a much more pleasant urban environment for pedestrians. *(Eddie Dixon/DMBC)*

An open-top tram, one of the first batch bought by the corporation, makes its way along Baxter Gate on this superb Simonton & Son card of *c.* 1905. The paperboys in the foreground appear more interested in the photographer than in the approaching tram. Two of the town's most spectacular commercial properties can be seen here: the splendid Clock Corner (Oriel Chambers, 1894) and Demaine and Brierley's Bank Chambers building with its impressive green-topped dome, originally created in 1898 for the York City & Commercial Bank (and more recently used by the Midland, now HSBC). Oriel Chambers was designed by the local architect and civil engineer J.G. Walker and was soon occupied by solicitors and the Sheffield Banking Company. By the late 1920s the commercial part of the building was used by Burton, the Leeds-based tailors. *(Chris Sharp Collection)*

It is well worth looking at buildings above eye-level in order to appreciate their architectural detail – though it is not easy to do on busy shopping days! Consider, for example, the upper part of Clock Corner, where the decorative stonework (in fine-grained sandstone from Crosland Hill quarries, Huddersfield) and landmark clock are prominent features. *(Author)*

An intrepid passenger hops off corporation trolleybus no. 24, with Hyde Park on its indicator, as it turns into St Sepulchre Gate. This vehicle, with its protruding cab and 'eyebrow' above the upper front windows, was one of twenty-two supplied to update and extend services by 1931. The racecourse route was started on 30 March 1930. The pavement outside Burton's shop at Clock Corner is extremely busy with shoppers. This is an Empire View card by Charles Jamson. *(Author's Collection)*

William Anelay snr (1841-1918) and his firm were responsible for new building and restoration work at numerous Doncaster area properties, including Rossington Hall (1882), St Mary's Church, Tickhill (tower restoration, 1882), St Wilfrid's at Hickleton (restoration work, 1883), Doncaster Free Library and Art School (1889), St Helen's at Marr (restoration, 1891), the new St Jude's Church, Hexthorpe (1894), St Wilfrid's at Cantley (restoration, 1894) and the new York City & County Bank (1898). The Anelays built up an excellent reputation, working with architects of both regional and national standing. *(Author's Collection)*

Carved figures and classical architectural features in expensive Portland stone grace the splendid dome of the Midland Bank building. The white façade is still bright after over a century of weathering and atmospheric pollution. *(Author)*

St Jude's at Hexthorpe, like neighbouring St James's, served many families associated with the GNR's Plant Works. Construction commenced in 1893 using Balby bricks and Acaster stone dressings in a Gothic style, and the building was financed principally by Lord Grimthorp (Edmund Beckett Dennison), his sister and a local resident, Mr Pybus. Dennison's sketches were converted into plans by Herbert Athron of Dolphin Chambers, Doncaster, and put into effect by William Anelay. The dedication ceremony was performed by the Bishop of Beverley on 2 June 1894. *(Author)*

This view of Baxter Gate was taken in the early 1900s when horse-drawn transport was still common, though there is also a good view of an ornate tram standard on the right of the photograph, by the gas lamp. Children add interest to the composition, especially the lad in the cap leaning over the barrow, next to Blackburn's clothier's shop with its window display of flat caps. *(Chris Sharp Collection)*

The inventor Revd Edmund Cartwright DD moved to Doncaster in the mid-1780s, after inheriting no. 22 Baxter Gate. He sought skilled artisans capable of building and working his power looms. Lacking financial support in Lancashire, he set up a spinning and weaving mill and then a four-storey factory, the machinery driven by water from the Don. The last venture was not successful, and Cartwright was crippled financially. Undeterred, Dr Cartwright sold his Doncaster factory in 1793 and moved to London where he invented an alcohol-powered engine. Later he carried out agricultural experiments for the Dukes of Bedford, and in 1809 was rewarded by parliament for his power loom which was acknowledged as being of national importance. He died at Hastings in 1823. *(Author's collection)*

29

Baxter Gate looks busy with shoppers in the 1950s. Some familiar businesses were already operating in the town: F.W. Woolworth, Boots the chemist and Owen Owen. *(Author's collection)*

St Sepulchre Gate. This card was posted in Doncaster on 18 August 1936, but the photograph was probably taken a few years earlier. We have a good view of three corporation trolleybuses, no. 13 (facing), no. 23 (nearest the camera) and no. 15. The trams have gone although the rails are still present on the road surface. The Portland stone buildings on the right of the photograph include The Central Chocolate Box (the former Nag's Head), Danum Chambers and the fine Montagu Burton building. *(Author's collection)*

Buildings, Businesses & People

Nowadays it is hard to imagine that such a fine and imposing building as the Guild Hall once graced French Gate. This is an E.T.W. Dennis of Scarborough card posted in Doncaster in 1904. *(Author's Collection)*

The old Guild Hall can be seen in its setting in this later card, dating from about 1928. French Gate (part of the Great North Road) is bustling with people and traffic. The tram tracks and overhead wires would still have been in use for the Bentley route which started here before running across the North Bridge. *(Norman Ellis Collection)*

The junction of Baxter Gate and St Sepulchre Gate is hardly discernable from the perspective of this excellent early photograph by Scrivens. A policeman directs traffic at the crossroads. We have a very good view of several businesses on the Clock Corner side: Boots the chemist, T.H. Oliver's and Burton's. *(Chris Sharp Collection/Old Barnsley)*

There is plenty of detail on this superb Scrivens photograph, taken from the end of High Street looking towards Clock Corner. The lady with the pram and the gentleman wearing a suit and cap (bottom right) watch the photographer as he composes the picture. A great deal of preparation was required to achieve such good results. Notice how the image is almost framed by a graceful street lamp on one side and the upper part of an ornate tram standard on the other. Good photographers needed the eye of an artist – along with flair, salesmanship and a great deal of hard work – to be really successful. Scrivens, like the even more illustrious Francis Frith, had all these qualities. *(Chris Sharp Collection/Old Barnsley)*

This late E.L. Scrivens card was sent from Doncaster on 4 September 1935. It provides us with an interesting view of the commercial buildings at the corner of High Street and Scot Lane: the attractive and recently completed (by Walter Brierley in 1925) Westminster Bank with its long classical façade of Portland Stone and the older Yorkshire Penny Bank with its new (1924) extension into High Street. In fact the sender's complete message read 'I thought you would like this card which shows the alteration in the Bank.' *(Author's collection)*

During the late Victorian and Edwardian period a visit to a photographer's studio was a popular activity. Technological advances and the boom in photography meant that working-class people were able to afford group and individual portraits. Research by Keith Adamson has shown that there were more than a dozen commercial photographers in town during the early 1900s. Understandably, High Street was a prime and busy location. F.J. (Francis John) Garrison of Goole established a photographic branch at 9 High Street in the 1890s, later moving to 14 St George's Gate (eventually with Deakin) and Printing Office Street. Here is an enlarged cabinet-size print from one of his early studios. Although the sitter is unknown, the name 'Mrs Beacock' is written in pencil on the back. *(Author's Collection)*

This cabinet print is from the studio of Arthur Rands, also of 9 High Street, though he is not listed in Keith Adamson's *Commercial Photographers in Doncaster* compilation (Royal Photographic Society Historical Group, 1982). However, not all photographers advertised in newspapers or were listed in trade directories. Again (and as usual!) the subject is not identified but on the reverse the very satisfied purchaser has written a note to the photographer, ordering '1 doz of these' and '2 doz of Post Cards', stating: 'they are very nice. Please do them as soon as you can. Yours Truly, M. Vasey. *(Author's Collection)*

Millions of small photographs known as *cartes de visite* were produced by Victorian and Edwardian professional photographers. Some studios were remarkably small, occupying terraced houses in suburban streets and village locations. This quality *carte* of a young child (never an easy subject!) is from the studio of Gottlieb Schroeder, who operated from 9 High Street from 1889 to 1893 and then from Scot Lane. When Schroeder died in poverty his fellow photographers collected sufficient money to pay his funeral expenses. *(Author's Collection)*

Making and printing customised 'blanks' for commercial photographers was a considerable business in its own right, and this example was produced by a Manchester company. The reverse of *cartes* and cabinet prints gave the photographer a great opportunity to advertise his studio(s) and boast about any famous subjects or commissions. Here, Schroeder claims to be 'Photographer to the Royal Families of England, Russia and Prussia' underneath impressive royal arms. Such claims were quite common and were often exaggerated, although Schroeder's Germanic origins may well have involved him taking royal photographs, though not necessarily commissioned ones. *(Author's Collection)*

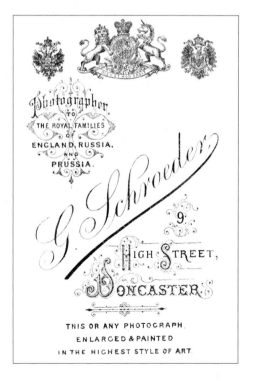

Doncaster and South Yorkshire owe a great deal to Edward Leonard Scrivens' 'real photographic' postcards covering the period from about 1908 to the Second World War. Here is another of his superb High Street images which offers so much detail for anyone interested in local and family history. Note, for example, the hand pointing to the garage of the Danum Hotel at the Cleveland Street junction; the policeman on point duty; the well-stocked glass and china shop at the Scot Lane corner and a host of advertising signs above street level including giant spectacles and flags. *(Chris Sharp Collection/Old Barnsley)*

The year on the postmark on this Mason's Alpha card of Doncaster High Street is not clear but the vehicles in the photograph, by J.F. Lawrence, suggest a mid- or late 1950s date. It provides us with a good view of the Danum Hotel and part of Hibberts' confectionery shop. *(J.F. Lawrence/Author's Collection)*

A wonderful early Scrivens card showing the new Danum Hotel, clearly a fashionable Edwardian edifice with its graceful attic storey windows, elegant dome and iron crest surmounted by a flag pole. This impressive but not overstated building replaced an old coaching inn, The Ram, in 1908–9. There was no canopy over the High Street entrance in those days. (*Author's Collection*)

South Parade and Hall Gate certainly represented the most elegant part of the Great North Road. Scrivens comes to our assistance in this composition which focuses on the north side of the road. The classical frontage of the purpose-built South Parade (later Majestic) Cinema, opened in 1920, catches the eye but it was rebuilt as early as 1933, becoming the Gaumont. *(Chris Sharp Collection/Old Barnsley)*

The very elegant and unusual war memorial of light brown sandstone was erected in 1923, coinciding with the opening of Elmfield Park. In the distance is the Town or Hall Cross, transferred from the top of Hall Gate to South Parade in 1793. *(Author's Collection)*

Several interesting late Georgian properties can be seen above street level on the south side of Hall Gate, near the Waterdale junction, in this 1994 photograph. The portico and steps of the former Francis Sinclair shop continue to be an attractive feature. *(Author)*

A trolleybus passes the Corn Exchange and through the market area on this postcard sent from Doncaster on 9 July 1952. (*Author's Collection*)

In the twilight of the trolleybus era: an interesting close-up of no. 371 in West Laith Gate, bound for Hexthorpe. It was one of nine 'utility' (wartime) vehicles later rebodied by Roe of Leeds with sixty-two seats. This vehicle was one of twenty-eight left in 1961 prior to the gradual run-down of the system. The Hexthorpe route was finally withdrawn in March 1962. (*Author's Collection*)

It is interesting to see how some buildings change their function over a relatively short period of time. Here, on Wood Street, is the old Doncaster Borough Education office, photographed on 20 July 1963. Its brick and stone façade, complete with a classical portico and hooded lintel, makes it an aesthetically pleasing building, and certainly an asset to the street. Next door, just visible, is the stationer's shop of Horace Pickering. Retired police officer Mr Alan Paley (b. 1926) told me that he started work here in 1940, earning 'ten bob' a week before becoming a police auxiliary messenger boy based at the Guild Hall. *(Alan Paley)*

The old Borough Education building is seen here in December 1994, shortly before its conversion into a public house/trendy Irish theme bar, known as Durty O'Dwyers. *(Author)*

In 2002 the Wood Street building was refurbished yet again and linked to Hall Gate as The Goose. *(Author)*

This unusual photograph shows part of the once-familiar Marsh Gate bus station area before the clearances of the mid-1960s. In the distance is the Bridge Hostel or Temple's Model Lodging House. *(Alan Paley)*

This later view shows the site of the old bus depot not long after the clearance of the terraced houses. This area was soon to be developed as a major dealership area for several motor vehicle companies. *(Alan Paley)*

A no. 23 corporation tram passes between St James's Church and the YMCA building on what is now Trafford Way. This was where the Balby and Hexthorpe routes diverged. Another tram can be seen making its way up the incline towards St James's Bridge on the left of the photograph, which probably dates from about 1902. (*Norman Ellis Collection*)

The YMCA building, which stood at the junction of St Sepulchre Gate and Cleveland Street, was demolished in the early 1960s. Built originally as a small hospital, its clock tower, decorated brick pediments at the roof gable and arched windows made it a striking feature at the edge of town. This postcard was published by Crowther of Rotherham and was sent from Doncaster in 1908. (*Norman Ellis Collection*)

This interesting view of High Street is from a postcard published by the Doncaster Empire View company. It was sent on 6 August 1946 but the photograph probably dates from the late 1930s. The oblique view helps us appreciate how the road curved elegantly to the right, following the line of the Roman road from York to Lincoln which bent towards the Danum fort on the site of St George's Church. (*Author's Collection*)

People & Occasions

There was a great deal of excitement in Doncaster on 3 October 1903 when Buffalo Bill's Wild West Show hit town – or more precisely Town Moor. More than 20,000 people are believed to have attended two spectacular performances, attracted by the prospect of seeing the legendary William Frederick Cody and his all-star cast. The logistics involved in staging the event were enormous. Cody's people, along with props and baggage, arrived in three trains. An arena was assembled and a vast multicultural village suddenly materialised: there were American Indians, Mexicans, Cubans, Cossacks and US soldiers, each group catered for according to ethnic and cultural need. The sideshows and miniature village attracted almost as much interest as the main event. After the evening performance the whole roadshow – some 500 players and helpers – packed up and moved on to Sheffield. *(Author's Collection)*

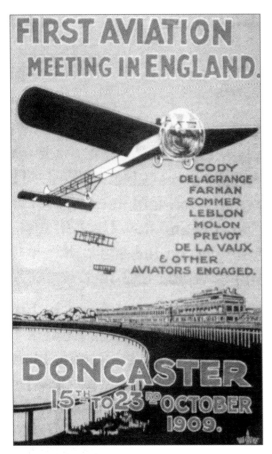

The first aviation meeting in England was held at Doncaster Racecourse between 15 and 23 October 1909, only a few weeks after the world's first aviation meeting at Rheims in France. The star was the American Colonel S.F. Cody who in his *Flying Cathedral* had recently achieved (albeit for just 27 seconds) Britain's inaugural powered flight at Farnborough. An opportunist who changed his name from Franklin Cowdery in order to cash in on the Buffalo Bill legend, Cody received a huge appearance fee of £2,000. The event certainly fired the public imagination, with about 100,000 people attending daily. Few were put off by the very real prospect of crashes. *(Author's Collection)*

Such was Cody's confidence and flair for publicity, that he responded to the *Daily Mail*'s offer of a prize for the first British pilot to complete a circular mile flight by signing British naturalisation papers in front of a packed grandstand. The band marked the occasion with a rendition of the *Star Spangled Banner* and the National Anthem. Sadly, Cody's British Army plane never got off the ground, sinking into the uneven ground while taxiing. The mishap was very disappointing for both the crowd and the organisers but did little to dent the showman's massive ego. *(Author's Collection)*

Monsieur Delagrange's Bleriot monoplane set a new world speed record at 49.9 mph. Notice the 'Women's Aerial League' banner displayed on the main grandstand in this high-quality postcard by Edgar Leonard Scrivens. *(Norman Ellis Collection)*

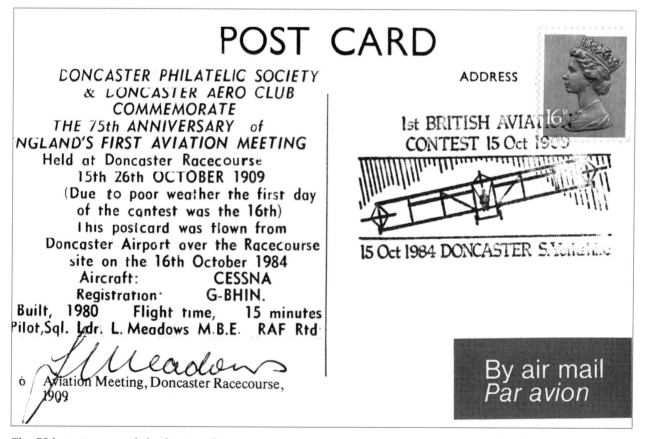

The 75th anniversary of the first British aviation meeting was celebrated in 1984. The original Delagrange postcard was reproduced by the Doncaster Philatelic Society and Doncaster Aero Club. To commemorate the event the card itself was flown from Doncaster Airport over the racecourse site in a Cessna. *(Author's Collection)*

Another successful flying machine was that piloted by another intrepid Frenchman, M. Roger Sommer, who made an astonishing flight of 29 miles in his Farman biplane, winning the new Doncaster Cup, donated by the Corporation of Doncaster. Proving that this was no fluke, he also received the Whitworth Cup for achieving the greatest distance (38 miles) in a day. (*Author's Collection*)

In total contrast, this jet aircraft was photographed at the last Finningley Air Show, held on a cold August day in 1994. One wonders if Doncaster's long aviation tradition will in future years include the building of an international airport at Finningley. Historic aircraft can now be seen at Aeroventure (South Yorkshire Aircraft Museum) at Doncaster Lakeside. (*Author*)

The delights of St Leger week always included an appearance by Tuby's funfair. The 'sensation of the year' appears to have been 'live teddy bears' as part of a small circus. Often referred to as *the* supreme showman, George Thomas Tuby (b. 1857) had six sons and four daughters. He was a popular town councillor and alderman in 1913 when this photograph is believed to have been taken. He served as mayor in 1921–2 (*see* p. 60). (*Roger Tuby Archives*)

Tuby & Sons' Scenic Palace ride in the early twentieth century. Any showman worth his salt would try to keep up with the latest technology – in this case the use of motor cars instead of the more traditional horses and other animals. (*Roger Tuby Archives*)

Resplendent in a fur coat and fashionable hat, HRH Princess Christian smiles at the crowd outside the Mansion House on Thursday 26 April 1906. She had come to open the bazaar in support of the Infirmary Fund, and the occasion was described by the *Gazette* as 'the greatest social and philanthropic event that Doncaster has witnessed for a great many years'. The princess, born in 1846, was the third daughter of Queen Victoria. The VIP welcoming party included the mayor, Councillor G. Smith, Lord Scarbrough and the Bishop of Sheffield. Town Clerk R.A.H. Tovey presented what appears to have been a very impressive illuminated address. *(Chris Sharp Collection/Old Barnsley)*

Doncaster police, territorials and a marching band stride from Hall Gate towards a packed High Street on Thursday 22 June 1911 to celebrate the coronation of George V. Scenes like this were repeated throughout the country at a time when the new monarch headed the largest empire in the world. This commemorative card also provides us with an interesting glimpse of the old properties at the east side of the Hall Gate/Silver Street junction. The gable end of Mr Pottergill's tobacconist's shop has been plastered with advertisements, including posters for the forthcoming appearance of Olive Lenton at the Grand Theatre. *(Norman Ellis Collection)*

The Mansion House and part of High Street festooned with decorations for a royal occasion, probably the coronation of George V. This image was skilfully produced by the Regina Company, press photographers of Printing Office Street. Even using modern equipment it is not easy to produce a good photograph of the Mansion House's impressive façade. (*Author's Collection*)

This superb early Scrivens photograph shows the Doncaster Mutual Co-operative and Industrial Society headquarters in Station Road elaborately decorated in celebration of the Royal Agricultural Show of July 1912. Graceful lamps illuminate the exterior ground-floor windows and pavement. Opened in 1897, the building had its own electricity supply, generated by a gas-powered engine. The Society boasted a membership of over 13,000 and annual sales well in excess of £314,000. (*Norman Ellis Collection*)

King George V and Queen Mary are welcomed by the mayor, Councillor W. Clark, at Doncaster station on 8 July 1912. This is one of a series of excellent views produced by the local Regina Company. (*Author's Collection*)

Doncaster's new North Bridge shortly after its official opening on 7 February 1910. What makes the photograph so appealing and interesting is the amount of detail included, particular in respect of the people and traffic captured in the scene. The leading open-top motor car accommodates three gentlemen in fashionable clothes, a lady and a driver wearing a light-coloured coat. The front-seat passenger is indicating a turn to the left, maybe via French Gate into Grey Friars Road, but the driver would have to take care to steer around the horse being led by a lady of fashion. The single tram line to the right led down into the depot. A grey horse is being led across the main road. We can also see bicycles and, several horse-drawn vehicles. The building near the crest of the bridge is the Brown Cow Inn, which had been rebuilt a couple of years earlier when George Reeson was the licensee. It was demolished in 1964. The distinctive three-storey stone building of white (Portland?) stone, with its rounded corner, formed part of the premises of F.G. Simpson's Farm and Garden Seeds emporium. The shop under the clock was occupied by William Burdet, watchmaker and jeweller. Next door we can just see George F. Hather's butcher's shop. (*Norman Ellis Collection*)

Doncaster's 'New Bridge', looking along French Gate towards the town. The old Volunteer Inn (the white-painted building) is clearly visible, just beyond the junction with Grey Friars Road. Further along on the same side is the junction with Lord Street which allowed access into the Volunteer Yard via Cheswold Street. Former local resident Alan Paley (b. 1926) recalls buying humbugs from 'old Mother Teale's' nearby shop when he was a lad. Probably originating in the mid-eighteenth century when it was known as the Skinner's Arms, the Volunteer was occupied in the early decades of the twentieth century by Joseph Sales who brewed on site. *(Chris Sharp Collection/Old Barnsley)*

This rare photograph, dated 19 November 1961, shows the North Bridge and in particular French Gate at a time when roadworks were taking place (prior to development) near the Grey Friars junction. The building on the extreme left is the old (*c.* 1892) public swimming baths, cleared about twenty years later. Almost next door is the Volunteer Inn, already closed and soon to be demolished. From the car park of the modern Tesco store it is now hard to visualise this interesting part of old Doncaster. *(Alan Paley/Cockayne)*

Joseph James Paley, a former police sergeant, was born at Crofton, Wakefield, in 1873, and was the tenant at the Volunteer Inn from 1939 to 1945. Wounded twice during the First World War (at Passchendaele and in Italy), his police career included spells of duty at Laughton Common, Ecclesfield, Darton, Edlington, Brighouse and finally Penistone. After the Volunteer, Joseph moved on to the Burn's Tavern (renamed Burn's Hotel) in Cemetery Road, Doncaster, and then to the Butcher's Arms at Swinton. Retiring in 1945, Joseph died at Hunmanby in North Yorkshire in 1973, aged eighty. *(Alan Paley)*

Ongoing major and complex engineering works has meant the closure of the old North Bridge to traffic until the summer of 2003. One of the final phases will involve the removal of pieces of the old bridge in sections as the new bridge is lowered into position. Work is also progressing to refurbish St Mary's Bridge over the Don. *(Author)*

Several private schools were established in Doncaster during Victorian times. Hall Gate School owed much of its success to William Toas Jackson, who served as headmaster from 1878 until his retirement in 1921. In the 1890s the basic curriculum included Latin, Greek, French, Drawing, Drilling, Singing and English. Parents paid extra for the teaching of German, Music or Shorthand. Boarders paid 12 guineas a term. This informal photograph, produced by the fashionable London photographic company Elliott & Fry, shows the smartly attired pupils in the exercise yard at the rear of the school. *(Author's Collection)*

This delightful studio photograph of Ivy Goodlad dates from 1916 when she was just sixteen years old and a senior pupil at Doncaster Girls' High School. It was probably a celebratory occasion for Ivy, dressed smartly in a distinctive outfit (note the hemline) but wearing her school hat. She was born at Staveley near Chesterfield where her father, Henry Goodlad, worked as a deputy and checkweighman at Seymour Colliery. The family moved to Woodlands, near Doncaster, in December 1907, Henry becoming a key worker and an official at the new Brodsworth Main colliery (*see* pp. 88–9). Ivy gained employment in the Doncaster Corporation Tramways' accounts department at the Grey Friars Road depot. *(Alan Paley)*

Most of the girls in this class at Bentley New Village Junior School were from mining homes. This photograph was taken in 1931, when there was a great deal of poverty among working-class families. Some of these children were soon to suffer the loss of a father or uncle in the terrible disaster at the local pit, on 20 November, when forty-five men were killed. Back row, left to right: Mona Orme, -?-, -?-, Doris Atkinson, -?-, Hilda Fisher, Annie Davies, Doris Hopkinson, Nellie Millington, Beryl Holmes, May Middleton; second row: -?-, -?-, -?-, ? Bellamy, Joan Scott, Alice Green, -?-, Edna Gerfin, Marjorie Mason, Marjorie Morley; third row: Betty Gordon, -?-, Freda Spiers, Alfia Eastwood, -?-, -?-, Betty Lee (?), -?-, Jessica Deakin, -?-; fourth row: Vera Large, Vera Button, -?-, Alice Gore, -?-, -?-, -?-; front row: Gladys Rowe, -?-, -?-, Evelyn Smith, -?-. *(Doris Kitching)*

An informal photograph of Warmsworth Church of England Reception Class, 1989. Back row, left to right: David Foster, Rachel Kelly, Alicia Large, David Hannah, Karl Moody, Alan Hibbins, Mrs Pomberth, Andrew Merrils and Gareth Richardson; middle row: Michael Handsford, Hannah Elliott, Sarah Wolsey, Lauren Evans, Elizabeth Kelly, Paul Jenkinson, David Williams, Katie Lapworth and Tim Hayes; at the front, kneeling: Charlotte Clayton and Louise Jones. Most of these children are now either in employment or further education and training. The school closed in the mid-1990s. *(Author's Collection)*

Profits of this Card

go to the War Relief Fund.

Printed from Joyful News Paper, Sept. 24th, 1914.

EDITOR .. ... REV. SAMUEL CHADWICK.

The Ministry of Song.

Doncaster is a city at present in the hands of the military. Everywhere the trim khaki-clad figure may be seen, and the people of the town have learned to know better the young fellows who are ready to go out for the protection of their country.

Mr. H. H. Roberts, Evangelist, whose home is in Doncaster, has composed the following lines after the pattern of " Where is my wandering boy to-night ? " to which tune he sings them in the public house, in the street, in the church, or anywhere where there are people to listen. Sometimes the audience—and this happened in the bar of a public-house—make a collection, which Mr. Roberts hands over to the Relief Fund. The Evangelist sings the song everywhere he goes, for everywhere there are those who have loved ones with the armies of the Allies.

The lines of the song are as follows :—

God bless our soldier-boys to-night—
The boys of our tenderest care,
The boys that are still our joy and light,
The boys of our love and care.

CHORUS.
The boys that have said " I'll go."
The boys that have said " I'll go " ;
God bless the boys who stand by the flag,
The boys that have said " I'll go."

God bless our sailor-boys to-night,
The boys we are proud to know,
The boys that have answered their country's call,
And gladly said ' I'll go."

God bless the mothers who mourn their loss,
The bairns who are fatherless,
The wives of our fighting soldier-boys—
Protect them, and guide, and bless.

God Save the King.

Cards obtained from 63, Morley Road, Doncaster.

This interesting postcard in the form of a song sheet was printed in 1914 from the *Joyful News Paper* (editor: the Revd Samuel Chadwick) in support of the War Relief Fund. Material such as this was locally produced in many towns and cities in order to encourage young men to 'answer their country's call'. *(Norman Ellis Collection)*

The small village church of St John at Cadeby was completed in about 1856 to the design of Sir Gilbert Scott, while he was also busy with a far larger commission, St George's at Doncaster. St John's has recently undergone a major renovation programme. Visitors to the attractive churchyard can see the grave of a Doncaster First World War hero, Lance Corporal G.H. Wyatt VC. *(Author)*

George Harry Wyatt, on leave from the army, is seen here receiving the congratulations of a police officer in St Sepulchre Gate, Doncaster. On 25 August 1914, at Landrecies, he dashed out of the line on two occasions, despite very heavy fire, in order to extinguish burning straw which threatened to make his unit's position untenable. A few days later, at Villers Cotterêts he received a head-wound but continued fighting until the flow of blood blinded him. After impromptu treatment he returned to the firing line and resumed combat. For these acts of exceptional courage he was awarded the Victoria Cross. After the war Harry joined the Doncaster Borough Police, attaining the rank of sergeant, and he remained a popular public figure for many years. (*Author*)

The grave of George Harry Wyatt VC (of the 3rd Battalion, Coldstream Guards) in Cadeby churchyard. (*Author*)

On Saturday 19 July 1919 peace parades took place throughout the country. The celebrations at Edlington were recorded in a series of picture postcards. 'No. 4' captures the occasion wonderfully. A farm horse and colourful dray pause for the photographer at the end of Victoria Road. The local vicar and men in their best suits, sporting trilbies or caps, stand or squat alongside smartly attired women wearing summer hats. Most of the group appear to be wearing peace ribbons, but what captures the eye is the splendidly decorated float and the dressed-up women and girls representing Peace and Victory. The little boy in fancy dress with his decorated bicycle adds interest at the extreme left of the image. The group formed part of a grand procession through the village and the day ended with a public bonfire. *(Norman Ellis Collection)*

Cheap and cheerful, peace mugs were produced nationwide in huge numbers as souvenirs of Peace Day. Many still survive and are of interest to collectors of commemorative pottery. This customised example would have been given to a child or participant in the Edlington celebrations, so is of considerable social importance. *(Author)*

A group of wartime workers and officials assemble for their photograph outside what is believed to be the old courthouse in Doncaster at Christmas 1917. The image bears the stamp of the Sansom Studios of Baxter Gate, Doncaster. The proprietor, Percy Sansom, was in business at no. 13 from 1913 to 1923 before moving to 1a St George's Street. *(Author's Collection)*

The 1918 General Election took place on Saturday 14 December. The Doncaster Division candidates were Mr R. Nicholson (Liberal) and Alderman R. Morley (Labour). Here we can see Reginald Nicholson outside the Mansion House, celebrating his election victory, on 28 December. The count had to be delayed in order to allow the processing of service men's and women's votes. Women aged over thirty voted for the first time, the occasion being described in the *Doncaster Gazette* as 'the entry into the polling booths of the newly enfranchised fair sex'. Research has shown that most women followed their husband's or a relative's views. Nationally, eleven million votes were cast, twice more than in 1910. The Coalition Government of David Lloyd George triumphed in the so-called 'Coupon Election' called immediately after the First World War. The 'coupon' tag was a reference to personal letters of endorsement sent by the Prime Minister to approved candidates. Only one woman was elected, Countess Markievicz, for a Dublin Sinn Fein seat but she refused to take the oath of allegiance to the king. This card was sent 'With Mr Nicholson's best wishes for a happy new year' to Mr Edwin Robinson of 47 Shady Side, Hexthorpe. *(Author's Collection)*

George Thomas Tuby (family motto: 'Whilst I live I'll crow') was a popular Mayor of Doncaster in 1921–2. Born at Long Newland, Selby, in 1857, the son of a Doncaster Plant Works railway worker, Tom rose to become one of the greatest travelling showmen of his cra and managed to combine this with a distinguished career in public life. His 'Infirmary Benefit' in the fairground during race week was a popular institution and as a member of the Board of Guardians he was well known for his generosity. In many ways a pioneer, he combined the traditional shooting galleries, coconut shies, penny peep shows, swings and roundabouts with innovative experiences such 'Whoa, Emma', a 'scenic railway' and the use of bioscopes, which introduced moving pictures to the masses. His year of office was rightly praised by the *Gazette* of 22 September 1922 and he was even invited by King George V to a party at Buckingham Palace in celebration of the forthcoming marriage of Princess Mary and Viscount Lascelles of Harewood. G.T. Tuby was the last mayor to live at the Mansion House although he preferred the comfort and flexibility of his caravan. When he died in 1932 the funeral cortège stretched for a quarter of a mile from his Copley Road home. *(Author's Collection)*

Mayor Tuby, his wife Maria and Princess Helena Victoria, who was on an official visit to Doncaster to open a YMCA bazaar in March 1922. *(Roger Tuby Archives)*

Tom Tuby's showman's traction engines were each named in celebration of his public life: *Councillor, Mayor, Alderman* and, in this splendid surviving example, *Ex-Mayor. (Roger Tuby Archives)*

G.T. Tuby's restored portrait was unveiled in a ceremony at the Mansion House as part of Festival 800 in 1994, marking the Showman-Mayor's contribution to the borough. Here we can see Tom's grandson George Thomas (right), who carried on the family's civic reputation as Mayor of Scarborough, and great-grandson Roger Tuby, who as Roger Tuby & Son Funfairs carries on the showman tradition. Anyone interested in the Tuby story and funfairs in general can visit their excellent website at www.rogertuby.co.uk. *(Roger Tuby Archives)*

This postcard, printed and published by R.L. Crowther of 10 Sunny Bar, was produced for the Bentley Labour candidate Joseph ('Joe') Robinson who was opposing Mr Massarella in the 9 April 1925 council elections. Joe had started work at Bullcroft colliery at the age of twelve and was a miner for an incredible fifty-eight years, retiring aged seventy. His granddaughter Doris recalls her grandmother making knee pads for him as he spent most of his shifts in cramped conditions at the coal face. On Sunday mornings he would don his best suit and, with watch and chain across his waistcoat, looked 'every bit like the lord of the manor'. Massarella, standing as an Indpendent, won Bentley with a majority of 281 (Robinson polling 117). There was 'a good deal of cheering, counter-cheering and booing' at the speech ceremony, according to the *Gazette*. *(Doris Kitching)*

A Bentley family spanning four generations: veteran miner Joe Robinson is seen here with his daughter Lily Wright (née Hopkinson), granddaughter Doris Kitching (née Hopkinson) and her children, Pauline and Norman, at a wedding at Bentley Church in the coronation year of 1953. *(Doris Kitching)*

An informal group photograph taken on the occasion of the wedding of Thomas Hopkinson and Lily Robinson in 1919. The happy couple (shown seated, with arms linked at the centre of the group) were married at St Peter's Church, Bentley. They spent the first few months of their married life in an old terraced house in New Street before moving to 35 Daw Lane, described by their daughter Doris as a 'light and airy' new council property, situated near the pit. Thomas was to lose his life in the Bentley mining disaster of 1931. *(Doris Kitching)*

A wartime wedding sixty years ago: Doris Hopkinson and Norman Kitching were married at Bentley Church at 3 p.m. on 18 April 1942. The vicar was the Revd Norman Campbell, who recalled that there was a marriage every half-hour during that day. The groom at the previous ceremony celebrated a little too early and was seen 'doing cartwheels on the church lawn' before proceedings commenced. Despite rationing, 'a good spread and a barrel of beer' was provided for sixty-five guests (including four sailors 'in whites') at the bridegroom's mother's house, Bentley Toll Bar. Doris and Norman, who met at a dance at the Bentley Pavilion, celebrated their diamond wedding anniversary in 2002. *(Doris Kitching)*

Floods at the locks, photographed from the North Bridge, May 1932. Thirty hours of torrential rain caused widespread flooding in the countryside around Doncaster during late May. Fields were turned into inland seas and whole villages and farmsteads isolated. Denaby pit was idle and Conisbrough cut off. Bentley Road was said to resemble Venice. At the North Bridge the canal water rushed over the upper gates of Marsh Gate lock and flooded nearby cottages. For those wanting to escape to the cinema, the main film at the Arcadia was *A Handful of Clouds*, starring Lew Ayres and James Cagney! *(Norman Ellis Collection)*

A local photographer captured this flood scene in the main street of Arksey in the early 1930s. Everyone seems quite cheerful despite the catastrophe and the Revd J. Pierce Price, wearing waders, is on hand to maintain morale. The flood waters extended to Bentley and Doris Kitching recalled the family piano being placed on its back on a table as it was far too heavy to carry upstairs. It stayed put for a month. The family returned home to an inescapable foul smell and a massive clean-up operation. The council supplied strong disinfectant to each home. *(Chris Sharp Collection)*

Monday 6 May 1935 was the official day for celebrating the Silver Jubilee of King George V and Queen Mary, and the occasion was marked by many thousands of street parties. Understandably, events nationwide were spread over several days. In this typical street scene, families gather in Upper Oxford Street, Doncaster, on Saturday 4 May. A few of the women wear 'pinnies' while young girls display their party frocks. Stretching the bunting across the street must have been a difficult task. This photograph is one of a series by the Lawrence Electric Studios. *(Norman Ellis Collection)*

It's 3 June 2002 and residents from St Peter's Road, Balby, celebrate the Golden Jubilee of Queen Elizabeth II with a traditional street party. *(Malcolm Billingham/Doncaster Free Press (SYN Ltd))*

The Mayor and civic dignitaries parade towards the Corn Exchange in War Weapons Week in Doncaster, 7–15 February 1941. Such occasions encouraged towns and villages to raise much-needed funds to support the war effort, in particular for ships and weapons. 'Launch to win' is one of the mottoes on the large poster. The war was now costing Britain £11 million per day. Two months later income tax was raised to 50 per cent in the pound in support of the war budget. *(Norman Ellis Collection)*

Young women played a crucial but often disregarded role on the Home Front during the Second World War. The Edlington Women's Messenger Corps provided a vital communication link in the the village's Civil Defence arrangements. They manned telephones and conveyed messages, often in difficult conditions such as during air raids and blackouts, and liaised between the Home Guard, ARP, First Aid Posts and the police. Back row, left to right: Revd Hewitt, Olive Worth, Vera Birch, Kath Whelan, Joyce Elgy, Lily Ackroyd, Margaret Wheat and Violet Satathwaite; front row: Jean Stevenson, Eileen Whitney, Gladys Stevenson, Francis Davison and Ethel Wynne. *(Derek and Marion Mould)*

Stanley Frith stands by Doncaster's no. 375 trolleybus at a South Yorkshire Transport Open Day on 31 March 1984. It was a nostalgic occasion, for more than twenty years earlier, on 14 December 1963, Stanley drove this vehicle on its last official journey on the Beckett Road route, when it was full of dignitaries and enthusiasts. This marked the end of the town's trolleybus system. This historic vehicle is now at Sandtoft Transport Museum. Stanley told me that the trolleybuses were awkward to drive for any newcomer since, like a tram, there was no clutch and the left foot was used to operate the accelerator and the right foot for the brake. It wasn't unusual, when contact was lost with the overhead wires, for drivers to get local people to 'shove you back under them'. *(Stanley Frith/Jonathan Gunn)*

Public access to one of the most historic sites in our area, Tickhill Castle, has been limited to an annual event in recent years. The Edwardians also enjoyed the opportunity to visit the castle grounds, as can be seen in this early postcard of the house within the inner bailey. *(Author's Collection)*

Tickhill Castle grounds full of visitors in April 1987. A year or so earlier an archaeological team from Manpower Services recorded details of the motte, bailey and curtain walls. On 9 June 2002, despite pouring rain, over 550 people viewed the grounds during the annual three-hour opening courtesy of the Duchy of Lancaster estate. *(Author)*

Doncaster's town cryer Mr Alec Corney entertains Tickhill Castle visitors, including my wife Angela and daughters Hannah and Natalie, in April 1987. The interesting and colourful history of Tickhill and its castle is told in Tom Beastall's excellent *Tickhill: Portrait of an English Country Town* (Waterdale Press/Doncaster MBC, 1989). *(Author)*

The aerial antics of the Groovy Gang entertain visitors as part of the Queen's Golden Jubilee celebrations on the Solar Plaza at the Earth Centre, Denaby Main, 3 June 2002. Other attractions included stilt walkers, Hope the Hare, balloon modellers, story telling in the Yurt (Exhibition Gallery), Living in the Past Duo, Priory Boys Brigade Band, face painting, Doncaster Scouts Marching Brass Band (below), the magic of Richard Rozel in the Castle View Conference Centre and performances from the renowned Doncaster Wheatsheaf Singers. Visitors could also embark on a Don cruise. It was a most enjoyable day despite the late afternoon downpour! *(Author)*

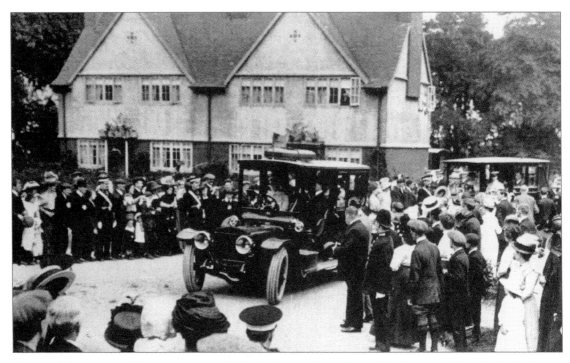

Residents of the new mining community at Woodlands greet King George V and Queen Mary during their visit on 9 July 1912. Scheduled into the occasion was a royal visit to a local property and the house of Brodsworth miner Henry Goodlad and his wife Emma Jane was duly chosen well in advance. Everything was spick and span, and the house had even been carefully redecorated. Unfortunately the royals were directed to the wrong house! William and Sarah Brown and their daughter Hilda May received some most unexpected guests, with Bill having had no time to wash his blackened face since he had just finished a shift at the pit! Back at the Goodlads, Henry and Emma were left puzzled as to why their visitors had not arrived. For the rest of his life Henry would often joke to his wife, 'Might as well take my tie off, he's not going to call, lass.' *(Alan Paley)*

On Wednesday 3 July 2002 opera singer Lesley Garrett returned to her home town to promote her first public performance in Doncaster. Originally from Thorne, Ms Garrett, seen here outside the Mansion House, was to star in the concert *One Singular Sensation* at Doncaster Racecourse on 21 July. Lesley was also in town to support the new theatre project and later joined the Commonwealth Games Baton Relay, running one of the legs through Doncaster. *(Doncaster Free Press (SYN Ltd))*

Entertainment & Employment

'Little Titch', real name Harry Relph, was one of the most popular of the music hall comedians. Along with the likes of George Formby and Dan Leno, he appeared at the Royal Opera House (Theatre Royal) in the Market Place (before its demolition in 1900) and then at the new Grand Theatre. Although only just 4 ft 6 in tall, he purposefully wore long boots as props for his hilarious antics, boots which so happened to accommodate his two extra toes on each foot. He also had a 'spare' finger to each hand. *(Author's Collection)*

Miss Agnes Sutherland and her amateur thespian pupils gave three Shakespearean performances, beginning with *The Merchant of Venice*, at the Guild Hall on 22–24 November 1911. The *Gazette* described the play as 'very commendable and entertaining' with Miss Sunderland, 'in the popular role of Portia', acting throughout 'with insight and vivacity'. There was also praise for Miss Esme Beckett, Miss Dorothy Bragg, Miss Eleanor Laybourn and Miss Gertrude Blackburn, while Margaret Sutherland was 'quite manly' as Lorenzo. The orchestral selections were by Mr J. Harvey and his band. Proceeds were 'to that worthy object, Doncaster Infirmary'. *(Author's Collection)*

A late Edwardian view of the rather grand façade of the Palace Theatre, also known as the Palace of Varieties, which once graced Silver Street. It provided popular live entertainment until late 1920 when it was converted into a cinema. Further improved to 'super-cinema' status, it offered popular entertainment during the 1930s. After the Second World War the Palace became the Essoldo and was one of the first in our area to to have a panoramic screen for the latest cinemascope films. The substantial building was demolished in about 1970. *(Author's Collection)*

The entrance to Central Hall snack bar, Printing Office Street, as it appeared on 4 June 1963. This interesting building, which opened on 12 April 1909, was utilised as a 350-seat cinema by James H. Tindle, described by local cinema historian Ron Curry as 'a picture pioneer of the North East'. Will Lincoln was manager and James H. Tindle junior operated the bioscope. G.H. Wright obtained a financial interest in the business in 1912 and by 1917 had embarked on a substantial contract (£17,000) for the establishment of a new Doncaster cinema. Six years later Wright was in debt and the pioneering Central Hall cinema closed. (Alan Paley/Cockayne)

Doncaster's first suburban picture house was built in just five months, and was opened by the mayor, Councillor Samuel Morris, on 5 September 1921. It boasted 720 seats and claimed to have 'the longest screen available' as well as the latest Western Electric Sound System. Its pebbledashed front and arched entrance provided a basic but distinctive façade. Between 19 and 21 May 1932 patrons could enjoy the film *Sally In Our Alley*, starring Gracie Fields, and the following week there was a double-bill of *Wicked* and *A Holy Terror*. There was a Saturday matinee, priced at 3*d* and 6*d*. Balby Cinema was sold to the Star Cinema Company in 1951 but closed nine years later. Until recently the building was used as a Far Eastern Food depot. (Chris Sharp Collection/Old Barnsley)

Situated in a good spot at the top of Hall Gate, the new Gaumont Palace was a large (1,800-seat) cinema, built in just nine months. Designed by the cinema architect W.E. Tate, and executed by contractors McLaughton & Harvey, it was opened by the Mayor of Doncaster, Councillor G.H. Raynard JP on 3 September 1934. The main film shown on the grand occasion was *Evergreen*, starring Jessie Matthews. The passing trolleybus is bound for the racecourse, a route that started on 30 March 1930. In 1973 the Gaumont was converted into a small multiplex of three screens and it was renamed the Odeon in 1987. (Norman Ellis Collection)

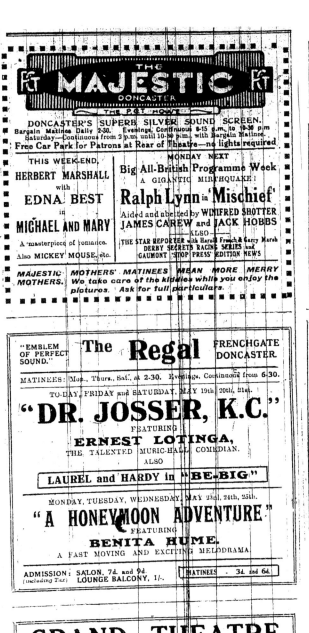

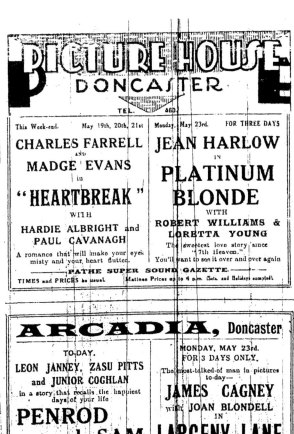

By the early 1930s there were five 'talking' cinemas in town, plus the new Balby Cinema in the suburbs. The loss of the Majestic in 1933 was more than compensated for by the opening of the Ritz on Hall Gate in November 1934, a deluxe 2,000-seat venue. By 1936 Ron Curry estimates that Doncaster had a cinema audience of 50,000 *per week* and there were seven new venues at nearby locations, providing another 10,500 or so weekly visits. Going to the pictures once or twice a week was, of course, not unusual. Here we can see advertisements for four town cinemas and for a live performance at the Grand, all published in the *Doncaster Gazette* on 20 May 1932. *(Author)*

A walk along the Don towards Conisbrough Castle was a popular leisure pastime for Edwardian Doncastrians and visitors. This interesting postcard was posted at Conisbrough in 1911. Ethel's message to her friend in Hull was: 'Arrived here at 4.30 pm. Hoping to see you at Strensall tomorrow evening.' A young girl appears to be purchasing an ice-cream from the mobile vendor at the castle gates. *(Author's Collection)*

This marvellous old photograph shows Mr Brown of Belmont Street, Mexborough, and his 'Pure Ice Cream' – along with his wife and children, posing a little awkwardly for the camera. Perhaps the grey pony was carefully chosen for its appearance and friendliness. *(Chris Sharp Collection/Old Barnsley)*.

This superb postcard of Hexthorpe Flatts by Scrivens was posted in Doncaster on 3 June 1928. Boating from this point on the Don was a popular pastime and a frequent subject for commercial photographers. But look how Scrivens has achieved not only a picturesque composition but plenty of human interest, and everyone, even the distant rowers, is looking towards the camera. *(Author's Collection)*

Three men in a boat . . . Jerome K. Jerome's humorous novel of this title was published in 1889 and its huge success may not have been forgotten when Scrivens took this photograph in the popular context of Sprotbrough Falls. One of the young men obliges by playing a ukulele. Again Scrivens has combined wonderful scenery with an interesting foreground. A few people are just visible on the opposite bank, by the abandoned keel boat – and just about everything is in sharp focus! *(Chris Sharp Collection/Old Barnsley)*

A Simonton postcard showing a very crowded sandpit at the Miners' Welfare Park, Bentley, perhaps taken on a Bank Holiday. *(Chris Sharp Collection/Old Barnsley)*

The Doncaster Dome, opened in 1989, serves as one of the largest leisure complexes in the country. It is a showpiece building, and materials such as glass and steel predominate in a wedding-cake style of architecture. The swirling outer staircase and the superb bronze of 'the swimmer' catch the eye. *(Author)*

Mr and Mrs Thomas Burkitt's well-stocked shop, situated next to Bentley Road post office, on a postcard sent from Doncaster in 1908. Rowntree's Pastilles and Clear Gums, Cadbury's Chocolate and Cocoa and Fry's Chocolate Creams are still familiar products almost a hundred years later but one wonders what happened to Watson's Matchless Cleanser & Polish, Fletcher's Indian Sauce, Fels Naptha Soap and Savondo Cleaner. Mr Burkitt also appears to have stocked Barrett's Liquorice Allsorts. *(Norman Ellis Collection)*

Many shopkeepers had a mobile trade, which was something of a necessity for Mr F. Pedley and his Hexthorpe Dairy. In addition to fresh milk, available 'twice daily', he also stocked eggs, butter, ice-cream and mineral waters. 'Dry' goods included biscuits and a variety of teas. His smiling wife and two assistants look on and the dappled grey pony must have been a distinctive asset on the main roads and terraced streets of Hexthorpe. Mr Pedley was obliging enough to display public and local notices in his shop window, one of them offering a £1 reward for a lost scarf and ring. The use of large frame cameras enable much detail to be seen with the help of a magnifying glass. This postcard was sent from Doncaster to Cambridge on 18 May 1905. *(Norman Ellis Collection)*

E. Bailey & Sons of 119 Bentley Road, Doncaster, specialised in new and second-hand furniture but also appear to have functioned as general dealers, with a mobile fruit and vegetable round. Notice the little girl placed in an orange box on the dray! *(Author's Collection)*

An interesting parade of shops at Doncaster Road, Balby. Within the space of a few yards you could obtain hardware, drapery items, baby clothes, pet supplies, confectionery, cycles (including spare parts), have a shave or haircut and have your boots repaired, and, for the more affluent, motor repairs were available. Although only a mile or so from town, such communities were almost totally self-contained and small businesses flourished, providing services and products both to local residents and to the increasing amount of passing trade. *(Chris Sharp Collection/Old Barnsley)*

There were many small Co-operative branch shops, like this example at King Edward Road, Balby, purposefully planned and strategically located at the end of terraced rows where delivery of dry goods such as flour could be made with relative ease. We can even see flour on the ledge of the first-floor goods entrance – and notice the protruding girder over the lintel where a pulley rope was placed to haul heavy sacks up into storage. As usual, children enliven an otherwise dull scene, especially the girl with the sleeping baby in a pushchair and the lad sitting in the barrow. This was yet another thoughtful Scrivens photograph that helps us appreciate our social and community history. The old Co-op branch is now a Nite & Day shop. *(Chris Sharp Collection/Old Barnsley)*

This aerial view of Hyde Park and the Hexthorpe area dates from 1963. We can see very contrasting housing areas. In the upper half of the photograph are the railway carriage and locomotive shops and the rows of terraced houses that were built by private enterprise for the Plant workers during the late nineteenth century. Nearer the camera are the multi-storey Corporation flats. *(Yorkshire Post Newspapers)*

Women munition workers employed by the Great Northern Railway are featured on this postcard from the Regina Company of Printing Office Street, Doncaster, dating from about 1914. The boy sitting at the centre of the second row may have been the son of one of the workers and looks smart in his suit and (borrowed?) flat cap. *(Norman Ellis Collection)*

Stone Close Avenue, Hexthorpe, in June 2002. This is one of a series of terraced rows developed by private landlords for railway workers during the late nineteenth century. Many of the houses retain their original façades. *(Author)*

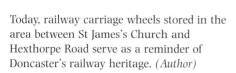

The Plant public house on Hexthorpe Road stood next to the railway carriage and locomotive works commemorated on the painted inn sign. *(Author)*

Today, railway carriage wheels stored in the area between St James's Church and Hexthorpe Road serve as a reminder of Doncaster's railway heritage. *(Author)*

My daughter Natalie and my friend Arthur Clayton, a former Barnsley area miner, pictured in 1989 at the commemorative pulley wheel marking the site of Denaby Main colliery. In the background is a South Yorkshire County Council notice relating to the Land Reclamation Scheme. In a hundred years (from 1868 to 1968) 203 of the mine's men and boy workers lost their lives. A plaque also commemorates the work of the late ex-Denaby pitman Jim MacFarlane who became Leader of Doncaster MBC in 1983 and was a lecturer in Industrial Studies at Sheffield University. Arthur Clayton started work as a boy of twelve and in later life became a noted local historian, researching and teaching in and around his home village of Hoyland Common. In June 2002 Arthur celebrated his 101st birthday. (*Author*)

Looking like a huge flying saucer but in fact carefully designed to reflect an old pit wheel, the Dearne Valley Leisure Centre was opened at the former Denaby Main pit site on Saturday 4 May 2002. The project was funded by Doncaster Council, Sport England and Dearne Valley City Challenge in order to meet the needs of surrounding communities, especially Denaby, Conisbrough and Mexborough. (*Author*)

Major bridge engineering works taking place near the troublesome railway crossing at Denaby Main, 3 May 2002. Massive improvements here will be much appreciated by private and public transport users, and the project serves as a further example of the continuing regeneration of the Don and Dearne Valleys. (*Author*)

This bronze statue of a grieving widow forms part of a moving tribute to the men and boys who lost their lives at the Cadeby and Denaby Main collieries, and also to the women 'who shared their lives and suffered their loss'. The sculpture, which stands in a public garden next to Conisbrough Library, is the work of Graham Ibberson and was commissioned by Doncaster MBC (with assistance from the art associations) in 1987. Behind the woman is part of a figure of a buried collier, one of his hands reaching desperately through fallen debris. (*Author*)

ASTER & DISTRICT RESCUE STATION.

Photographs of Mine Rescue Teams are quite common but this formal example, taken outside the Doncaster & District Rescue Station, is exceptional in its detail. The team members are displaying their 'Proto' breathing apparatus and associated equipment including a small canary cage. The Doncaster Mines Rescue Station was established in 1904, only two years after the first station in the country was opened at Tankersley, near Barnsley. It functioned from a handsome purpose-built building located at the junction of Wheatley Hall Road and Wentworth Road. Sadly, this structure, so important in our recent social history in terms of events such as the colliery disasters at Bentley, Hatfield and Lofthouse, was demolished a few years ago. Rescue workers from here retrieved bodies from the terrible chemical disaster at the Nypro plant at Flixborough in June 1974. *(Norman Ellis Collection)*

Yorkshire Main colliery photographed from the pit yard by Lamb & Company of Barnsley, from a postcard sent on 26 September 1923. Mineral rights near the village of Edlington were obtained by the Staveley Coal & Iron Company of Derbyshire in 1907 and the sinking of the colliery, initially known as Edlington Main, soon began. There were two shafts and the lucrative Barnsley Seam was reached at a record depth of 905 yards in July 1911. By 1927 the company was employing an underground workforce of about 3,000 men with another 500 on the surface. Many of the employees lived in New Edlington, a village specially created by the Staveley company, with leisure facilities that even boasted an open-air swimming bath. Before nationalisation in 1947 Yorkshire Main was part of Staveley's Doncaster Amalgamated Collieries group, along with Brodsworth, Bullcroft, Hickleton, Markham and Firbeck. (*Norman Ellis Collection*)

Not to be forgotten: Yorkshire Main closed in 1985 and the surface buildings were cleared. A half pulley wheel now marks the entrance to the Yorkshire Main Working Men's Club and sportsground. A smaller wheel can be seen on the old pit site near the modern Yorkshire Main Officials' Club at Edlington with a plaque bearing the following dedication: 'To those who died in accidents here or whose lives were shortened by disease or sickness and to their wives and families. Their contributions to the energy needs of the nation and the development of Edlington must not be forgotten.' (*Author*)

Wearing their summer uniform in the days when there was always a bobby on the beat are the men of Edlington Section (Doncaster Division) of the West Riding Constabulary, winners of the First Aid trophy from Yorkshire Main colliery. Back row, left to right: PC Bilby (Wadworth beat) and an unknown first aid man; front row: PS 464 Joseph Paley (in charge of section), PC 'Monty' Yeomans (Braithwell beat), PC Linton (Edlington beat), PC Walter Savage (Warmsworth beat) and PC Osborn Goddard (Edlington beat). The photograph was by G.S. Sullivan of Don Studio, St Sepulchre Gate, and was taken in 1938 outside the police station. *(Alan Paley)*

A large number of pickets meet a large force of police at the NCB's Coal House (now the Council House) in Doncaster on 26 March 1984 during the early days of the miners' strike. There were some ugly clashes on this occasion. *(Arthur Wakefield)*

The sod-cutting ceremony at Brodsworth Main, 23 October 1905. The ceremony was performed by the estate owner's wife, Mrs Thellusson of Brodsworth Hall. The person arrowed is Henry Goodlad, a miner and checkweighman from the Staveley Iron & Coal Company. The Staveley Company shared the costs of sinking two shafts with the Hickleton Main Colliery Company in a venture under the formidable chairmanship of Arthur, later Sir Arthur, Markham. The Barnsley seam was reached in October 1907 at a depth of 595 yards and production began on 26 November 1907 when 57 tons were extracted. By the 1920s a third shaft was sunk and production soared to over 6,000 tons per day. Brodsworth had become the biggest pit in Yorkshire and the most successful pit of its kind in the country. Soon, a series of world records were claimed for coal-drawing, each successively broken in some style. In 1957 Brodsworth Main, employing 3,600 men, produced 34,422 tons of coal during Bull Week – a new output record for what the *Yorkshire Evening News* described as Yorkshire's 'King's Pit'. *(Alan Paley)*

Henry and Emma Jane Goodlad pictured on their Golden Wedding Anniversary in 1935. Henry was the first man to be signed on as an underground worker at Brodsworth Main in 1906 and with his wife was one of the first residents in The Park area of Woodlands. After a short period working underground Henry was appointed as a deputy and then as checkweighman (as miners' representative). He was appointed agent of the Brodsworth branch of the West Riding Permanent Miners' Relief Fund, based in a sinker's hut on the bank, serving up to 3,000 members for twenty-seven years. A keen sportsman, Henry was a founder member of Brodsworth Main Working Men's Club, the colliery's brass band and its football and cricket clubs. He died in 1956, aged eighty-nine. *(Alan Paley)*

Brodsworth Main closed in 1990 and signs of the famous colliery were quickly erased from the ancient landscape (a Roman road ran between Woodlands and the pit). Gary Goodlad sits on the concrete plug covering the main shaft at the Brodsworth pit site. In 1991 Gary was appointed as HM Principal Inspector of Electrical Engineering in Mines, responsible for the enforcement of the law relating to health and safety within what remains of the mining industry. Gary is no stranger to Brodsworth Main. He is a grandson of Brodsworth veteran Henry Goodlad and served as a student apprentice (electrical) there from 1963. He was appointed as colliery deputy engineer at Markham Main, Armthorpe, in 1970, before joining the HM Inspectorate of Mines and Quarries, working in the South Wales Coalfield. Thus, remarkably, there was a Goodlad at the start and at the end of Brodsworth Main. *(Alan Paley)*

Denaby Main St John Ambulance Band. First Aid competitions and brass bands were encouraged by the colliery companies since health and safety were important issues both at a voluntary and statutory level. No doubt many of these men and their families were affected by the evictions of 1869, 1885 and 1902/3 when the Denaby and Cadeby Colliery Company withheld the houses of workmen who dared to question their authority. The so-called 'Bag Muck' strike of 1902/3, as Jim McFarlane has rightly shown, dominated the thoughts of local people for many years and stories were passed down the generations even to the present day. *(Author's Collection)*

One of the last great Yorkshire Miners' Demonstrations and Galas took place in Doncaster in June 1994. Here, at an early stage in the march, members and families of the Armthorpe Branch enter St Sepulchre Gate. *(Norman Ellis)*

A mass of colourful banners and bands pass along High Street during the 1994 Miners' Demonstration. *(Norman Ellis)*

A veteran Frickley miner pictured at the 1994 Miners' Gala defiantly displaying his home-made placard in protest at the recent closure of his pit. On the reverse are the words: 'FROM HULL, HELL AND HESELTINE MAY THE GOOD LORD DEFEND US.' *(Norman Ellis)*

This Charles Jamson photograph shows ice-cream workers at the Masserella factory in Hunt Lane (Bentley Town End), *c.* 1950. These premises formerly functioned as a roller-skating rink. Norman Kitching is outnumbered by the female workers. He recalls being bundled into a van and almost stripped naked by the ice-cream ladies by way of a welcome to the job! *(Charles Jamson/Norman Kitching)*

At the Earth Centre, Denaby Main, an elderly man, probably a retired coal miner, and two young children examine the spectacular exhibit called The Story of a Valley on 3 June 2002. Find out more about the Earth Centre on the Internet at www.earthcentre.org.uk. *(Author)*

Sport for All

Anita Chapman taking aim during archery practice at Cantley Sports Ground (Cases) in 1995, in preparation for the Atlanta Paralympics where she won an individual silver medal and a team bronze. This was astonishing progress for someone who had only taken up the sport, with husband Bernie, just two years earlier. The demanding event involved shooting six dozen arrows at a 70-metre target, followed by 'shoot-offs' against individual competitors. In the final contest Anita lost to an archer from Poland. *(Eric Hepworth)*

Anita Chapman was determined to avenge her defeat by her Polish rival though they remained the best of friends. She succeeded at the Sydney Paralympics, winning the gold medal by 13 points and also gaining a silver team medal. Thus in two Olympics Anita had achieved a gold, two silvers and a bronze medal. What an achievement! Here, Anita is holding her medals from the highly praised Sydney event which received international media coverage. Her final ambition, before competitive retirement, will be to represent Great Britain at the 2004 Athens Paralympics. Anita and her husband Bernie are members of the Harvester Archers Archery Club. New members including complete beginners are always made welcome; club contacts and details are available at Doncaster Library. (*Author*)

The Doncaster Rovers team, 1957/8. Back row, left to right:
Makepeace, Graham, Burgin, Kilkenny, Williams and Hopkinson;
front row: Mooney, Nicholson, Tindill, Cavanagh and Walker.
Centre-half Charlie Williams was to gain fame as comedian and
television personality and although he had left the club some
time before I was on the playing staff in the early 1960s his
antics on and off the field were already legendary.
(Author's Collection)

One of a series of fifty cards issued by Cadet Sweets in 1957, this
one features Doncaster Rovers' most exciting young player,
inside-left Alick Jeffrey. Alick was selected by Peter Doherty to
play in the first team when he was only fifteen years old. He had
scored thirteen goals in fifteen appearances at the start of the
1956/7 campaign but disaster followed. He broke a leg when
playing for the England Under-23 team against France, in
Bristol, on 17 October, prematurely curtailing his Football
League career. He made a remarkable comeback, after protracted
legal negotiations, during the 1963/4 season. Alick's appearance
in the reserves on 14 December attracted a crowd of almost
3,000 and nearly 12,000 greeted his debut at Belle Vue two
weeks later. As a young apprentice professional I trained and
played in practice matches with Alick during the difficult period
when he was trying to get fit. Admired by Stanley Matthews and
earmarked for signing by Manchester United's Sir Matt Busby,
Alick could have become a great international footballer.
(Author's Collection)

Doncaster Rovers, under new manager Mr Oscar Hold, parade for a pre-season photograph at the start of season 1962/3. Only a handful of players had been retained from the previous campaign, Hold managing to recruit a number of key players from bigger clubs including Eire international Alfie Hale and young goalkeeper Fred Potter, both from Aston Villa, and the veteran Liverpool captain Dick White; also signed was another veteran, Ray Sambrook from Manchester City. Back row, left to right: Wright, Billings, Helliwell, Potter, McCall and Fairhurst; middle row: Frank Marshall (asst trainer), Hinton, Lovell (kneeling, an apprentice), Robinson, Wales, Windross, Bratt, Herrington, Hildreth, Thompson, Taylor, Oscar Hold (manager) and Lew Clayton (trainer); front row, seated: Johnson, Ballagher, White (captain), Hale, Sambrook and Raine; on the ground are apprentices Stirling, McMinn, Elliott (the author) and Glover. The first team are wearing the new-style shirts with an extra white band. Other newcomers recruited during a remarkable season of signings for a Fourth Division club included Tony Conwell (Derby County), Keith Ripley (Peterborough), Denis Windross (Darlington), John Nibloe (Stoke), the much-travelled Albert Broadbent (making a return to the club from Lincoln City) and record signing Colin Booth, ex-Wolves and Nottingham Forest. Despite the investment the season started poorly, then there was a period of improvement that was interrupted by the worst winter since 1947. Only one game was played between the end of December and the beginning of March. I remember helping to clear the Belle Vue ground of snow, along with many other volunteers, for a home fixture against Stockport which we unfortunately lost 1–2, and indoor training sessions at RAF Finningley's gym. The season was extended because of the immense backlog of fixtures, Rovers finishing in a disappointing 16th position. But attendances averaged over 6,300 per home game and sharp-shooter Colin Booth scored thirty-four goals in forty-five appearances. (*Author's Collection*)

Colin Booth, pictured here as a Wolverhampton
Wanderers player (left) and shortly after signing for
Doncaster Rovers for a club record fee of £10,000. Born
in Manchester, Colin was a former England schoolboy
international and first made a name for himself as an
inside-forward with Wolves. Rovers transferred Colin to
Oxford United towards the end of the 1963/4 campaign,
shortly after the appointment of Bill Leivers as player-
manager, apparently making a profit on the deal.
(*Author's Collection*)

Harry Gregg made his debut for Doncaster Rovers in January 1953 but made
only occasional appearances over the next couple of seasons, deputising for
Ken Hardwick. In season 1955/6 he established himself as the first-team
goalkeeper and his potential was recognised when he was signed by
Manchester United in December 1957 for a Rover's record fee of £25,000 – in
fact the most ever paid for a goalkeeper. Described on the back of this card as
'a giant, flame-haired Irishman', Gregg went on to make 247 appearances for
United and was highly regarded for his heroics in the Munich air disaster
when he rescued a woman and her baby from the wreckage. He gained
twenty-five caps for Northern Ireland and was voted the best goalkeeper in the
1958 World Cup Finals. (*Author's Collection*)

Rod Johnson is described on the back of this 'My Favourite Soccer
Stars' card (presented free with the *Lion* comic) as 'a midget in stature
but a big favourite at Doncaster for his fast, fearless work as a striker
and sharp-shooter'. Johnson was signed from Leeds United by George
Raynor in 1968. During 1968/9 Rod was a regular in the Rover's
Fourth Division Championship team under new manager-coach Lawrie
McMenemy. (*Author's Collection*)

In April 1909 Mexborough heavyweight boxer William 'Iron' Hague knocked out Gunner Moir in the first round of a scheduled 20-round contest at the National Sporting Club to become the British champion. As a new 'white hope', Hague was fancied to take on the Americans, even Jack Johnson, for the world title. A small but significant hurdle was the 5 ft 6 in tall American Sam Langford who had lost only six times in eighty-nine contests. Langford was paid £2,500 for the fight and Hague received £1,800, substantial purses at the time. Although Langford was knocked to the canvas in the first round, a flurry of punches in the fourth put paid to 'Iron' Hague's world title aspirations. Hague's last big fight was in 1911 at the National Sporting Club when – despite training seriously for the first time – he lost his British title in the sixth round to Bombardier Billy Wells. *(Chris Sharp Collection/Old Barnsley)*

Popular Doncaster heavyweight boxer Bruce Woodcock (on bicycle) at H.O. Smith & Sons, cycle agents, 63–65 Copley Road, *c.* 1950. Born in 1920, Bruce represented the LNER at the Corn Exchange in 1933, when he was billed as the 'Schoolboy Champion of Yorkshire'. After a series of successful contests Woodcock was matched against Jack London in July 1945 when he became the first Yorkshireman since 'Iron' Hague to win the British heavyweight crown. A crowd of 60,000 attended the Jack Solomons world title promotion at the White City in June 1950 when Bruce met Lee Savold but the Doncaster man had to retire in the fourth round with a badly cut eye. *(Chris Sharp Collection/Old Barnsley)*

Stainforth Football Club, almost certainly composed of young mine workers, in season 1913/14. Quite a crowd can be seen assembling behind the goal area. The player standing on the extreme left and the trainer on the right both wear a neck scarf, a feature that I have also noticed on similar pre-First World War football photographs. The club mascot, sitting between the captain's legs, adds further interest. *(Author's Collection)*

Amateur football and cricket continued to be very popular during the inter-war period. Most larger works had one or more teams competing in local leagues. This is the Doncaster Tramway soccer team, season 1930/1, who played in the Thursday Amateur League. Back row, left to right: Scholey (sec.), Cuffling, Coults, Heap, Mellor, Holmes and Keyworth (trainer); front row: Fletcher (captain), Frith, Dennis, Snell, Horton and Davies. The photograph was taken before a friendly game against the Yorkshire Traction Company which resulted in an 8–2 victory for the 'Tramways'. *(Stanley Frith)*

Parading their new kit, this is the Edlington Secondary Modern School football team of 1947/8. Derek Mould recalls that the team's old black and amber kit had looked in a poor state in an earlier newspaper photograph, prompting several fund-raising schemes, including empty jam jar collections and a concert featuring young Jimmy Hodgson in a miners' sketch singing *Keep the Home Fires Burning*. Two new kits were bought from the proceeds and when they arrived at the school the senior team was hastily gathered together for a celebratory photograph – but there was no time for anyone to go home to get their football boots! Back row, left to right: Eric Reed, Mr P. Turton, Joe Jeavons, Roy Silman, Dennis Wheat, Terry Boothman, Mr B. Shaw (headmaster) and Billy Millward; seated: Edgar Chapman, Peter Bendle, Derek Mould, Ron Flowers and Les Stone. Two players went on to play professionally, Ron Sillman of Rotherham United and Ron Flowers who was a member of the great Wolves team of the 1950s and gained numerous England international caps. *(Derek Mould)*

A mud-spattered motorbike rider is superbly captured by the lens of Doncaster photographer Eric Hepworth during a British motocross championship round, organised by the Thorne & District club and held at Marshall's quarry, Dunsville, in December 1991. (*Eric Hepworth*)

This fine Scrivens photograph shows a packed racecourse and grandstand in about 1930. Two policeman are just visible in front of the riders and horse no. 20 appears to be heading towards the winner's enclosure. *(Norman Ellis Collection)*

The crowds are shown 'Leaving the Course' on foot and in a variety of vehicles on this late Edwardian postcard. The racecourse tram route opened at the end of June 1902 and the terminus by the stands in Grand Stand Road was planned with a loop so that trams could move off quickly, without having to reverse. In the busy September race week the trams on this route worked flat out, carrying punters to and from the course. *(Norman Ellis Collection)*

Lester Piggott (right) in the winner's enclosure during race week at Doncaster, photographed by a police officer on duty, Alan Paley, 10 September 1958. Christopher Darling, writing in the *Gazette*, described how one policeman had covered his hand with tips written in ballpen ink, but in the St Leger the hot favourite Alcide, ridden by W.H. Carr, was an easy winner. *(Alan Paley)*

Arthur Wharton is now generally regarded as the first black footballer. He was also a world-class athlete. Born at James Town, Ghana, in 1865, he began his sporting life as a goalkeeper for Darlington and attracted attention because of his unorthodox style. He moved to Preston North End, playing cup games for the famous 'Invincibles' but eventually settled in South Yorkshire. Between 1886 and 1887 he held the AAA 100-yards title, and was regarded as the 'fastest man on earth'. He set a British record of 10.00 seconds at Stamford Bridge. Wharton married and settled in South Yorkshire, playing for Rotherham Town and Sheffield United. His last known game was for Stockport County in 1902. He died in 1930 and was buried, virtually forgotten, in Edlington Cemetery. His life story has been chronicled in Peter Vasili's 1998 book *The First Black Footballer* and a film has now been produced about his remarkable life. *(Author's Collection)*

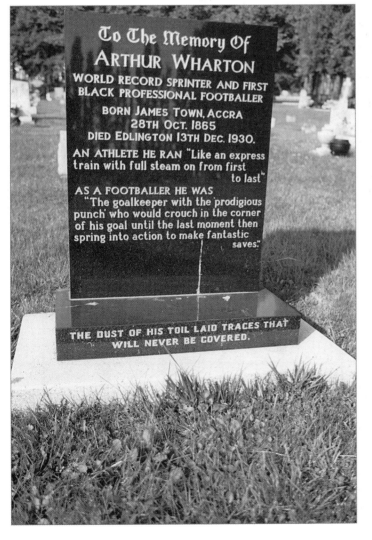

A modern headstone was placed on Arthur Wharton's grave in Edlington Cemetery in 1997, sixty-seven years after his death. *(Author)*

Doncaster Belles Ladies Football Club was founded in 1969 (as the Belle Vue Ladies) by a group of women who sold Golden Goal tickets for a Doncaster Rovers FC promotion. They have now become one of Britain's leading women's soccer teams (and founder members of the National League), winning many regional and two national titles. This is the 2001/2 team. Back row, left to right: Lizzie Gomersall, Jo Torr, Leanne Hall, Dani Petrovic and Karen Walker; middle row: Kevin Minchen, Becky Easton, Vicky Exley, Sarah Abrahams, Stacey Copeland, Melanie Garside, Gail Boreman and Sheila Edmunds (physio); front row: Aran Embleton, Laura Humphries, Gemma McCool, Julie Chipchase (manager), Karen Burke, Mandy Lowe and Claire Utley. Their home ground is Brodsworth Welfare in Welfare Road, Woodlands.
(FAOPL/Doncaster Belles)

Action at the Armthorpe ground in September 1996 when the Belles got the better of Ilkeston Town by four goals to one. Gill Coultard (left) and Tracey Kilner challenge for the ball. (*Eric Hepworth*)

Gill Coultard, the Belles' most capped player, and supporters with the Yorkshire Cup, 2001. Gill joined the club as a thirteen-year-old in 1977 and twenty years later had become the first women's footballer to win a hundred international caps. She also captained her country. (*Martin Sill*)

Doncaster Belles' current manager and former player Julie Chipchase. The Belles' official website can be visited at http//:www.donny.co.uk/Belles. (*FAOPL/Doncaster Belles*)

Action at Millmoor (Rotherham United's ground) during a cup semi-final in December 1995 when the Belles lost 1–2 to Arsenal. Karen Walker (centre) is challenged by Arsenal's Michelle Curley. *(Martin Sill/Doncaster Belles)*

The Belles beat Everton 4–1 in a league game at Brodsworth in September 2001. Maureen Marley (no. 5, Everton) and Jody Handley (no. 11, Belles) are in the foreground. *(Martin Sill)*

A young Rebecca Hudson in action at Wheatley Golf Club, *c.* 1995. In June 2002 Doncaster's golfing star won the Ladies' British Amateur Championship for the second time in her career and was also selected for the Great Britain and Ireland Curtis Cup team. Still only twenty-three, she has a great sporting future which could well extend to professional level. *(Eric Hepworth)*

How's that?! Bowler Nick Cowan appeals during a 1990s Doncaster CC fixture against Castleford. *(Eric Hepworth)*

The building of large leisure centres in recent years has meant that some indoor sports have been able to develop much more and also attract a good following – and a reasonable amount of sponsorship. During the early 1980s Doncaster had a basketball team capable of competing at the very highest level in the national men's league at a time when television coverage was widening interest in the sport. This excellent action shot by Eric Hepworth was taken at the Concorde Leisure Centre in Sheffield during season 1982/3 when Doncaster (sponsored by John Carr) played Warrington (FSO Cars). Norman Francis (13) attempts a basket, watched by team mates Bob Martin (6) and Dave Butler (10). *(Eric Hepworth)*

Willie Carson was always a popular jockey when he appeared on the Doncaster racecourse. In November 1991 he steered favourite Hieroglyphic to a one-length win in the last flat race of the season. *(Eric Hepworth)*

Doncaster RUFC's captain Richard Senior and supporters celebrate gaining promotion to the National North Division 2 at the end of the 1996–7 season. *(Eric Hepworth)*

A Dons player in action on a muddy Tattersfield in the early 1990s. The Dons had played at Bentley Road since 1953, the ground being named after their late chairman Len Tattersfield. The early to mid-1990s was a period of mixed fortunes for the club. They won their first trophy, beating Sheffield Eagles in the South Yorkshire Cup, and gained promotion to Division One but by the end of their first season the club had been placed into administration. The last game at Tattersfield was on 23 April 1995. Now 'breathing fire' as the Doncaster Dragons at Belle Vue, the club is now working in partnership with Doncaster Belles, Doncaster Rovers and the Council in bidding for a new community stadium for the town of Doncaster. *(Eric Hepworth)*

New Doncaster

Local schoolchildren assemble in Baxter Gate during the 1994 Doncaster Festival, displaying a variety of colourful banners specially created to represent aspects of the town and district's heritage. This was part of a community consultation process at an early stage of the Council's innovative Quality Streets programme, aimed at improving the environment of the town centre. Close cooperation with business and retailers resulted in a positive and effective working partnership for all involved. *(Neil Firth/DMBC)*

The participation of children, teachers and planners in a series of workshops in July 1998 resulted in some superb design elements that were incorporated by professional artists into the Town Map and Time Capsule. *(Neil Firth)*

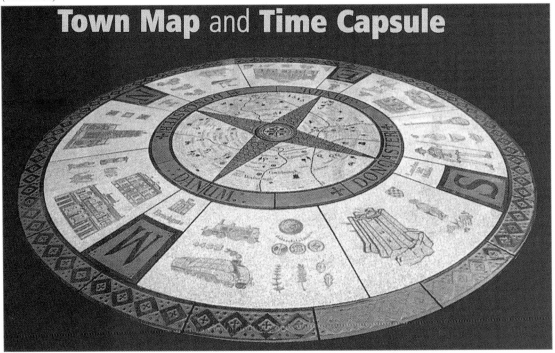

The Town Map and Time Capsule was completed in etched granite and inlaid resins by public artists Brian Jackson and Lesley Fallais, who co-ordinated the street and art workshops involving the people of the Borough of Doncaster. *(DMBC)*

The Mayor of Doncaster, Councillor Yvonne Woodcock, and a schoolboy lay the Time Capsule in a ceremony held in French Gate on Easter Monday, 5 April 1999. All the children involved in the project were presented with certificates at a Quality Streets celebration day at the Mansion House. *(DMBC)*

Public artist Hamish Horsley (wearing shorts) and his colleague, who is carving one of the Portland stone plinths, designed the Gillot Bar gateway. Doncaster Council employees Paul Bell (with spirit level and trowel) and Peter Cox (kneeling) are assisting with the construction work. This photograph was taken from Printing Office Street, looking towards the French Gate entrance. *(Neil Firth)*

The newly completed Gillot Bar at the entrance to St Sepulchre Gate, with the shaped stone and carved features of the work enhanced through illuminations and the photographic expertise of Eddie Dixon. We are also reminded of the Co-op's Living department store, soon to be closed and occupied by T.J. Hughes. *(Eddie Dixon)*

Printing Office Street, photographed by Eddie Dixon shortly before the commencement of Phase Two of the Quality Streets initiative in this area. We can also see shopfitters transforming the old Curtess shoe shop for Grafton's (bakers and confectioners), and the premises next to the Klick photographic branch has yet to be converted into the Morgans of Doncaster Eaterie. Also note the fine architectural details on the old Benefit Boot & Shoe Company building (above Grafton's). *(Eddie Dixon)*

A close-up of part of Gillot Bar, looking towards Printing Office Street, with the specially created Performance Area in the distance. The benches in Cadeby stone and granite are by Mike Disley. *(DMBC)*

A group of Doncaster MDC commissioned artists standing by one of the High Street tree sculptures, 29 May 2000. They are (left to right): Brian Jackson, Lesley Fallais, Victoria Brailsford, Richard Perry (tree sculptor) and David Mayne. Several professional public artists/facilitators were chosen for the task by Doncaster MBC following portfolio presentations of their work and workshops with local children. *(DMBC)*

The streetscape of High Street did little to enhance Doncaster's most elegant building and the façades of neighbouring properties, nor was it very friendly or interesting for pedestrians as we can see in this photograph taken on a wet day towards the end of 1998. *(Eddie Dixon)*

A much pleasanter and more interesting urban environment and civic space was created when Phase Four of the Quality Streets programme was completed in late 1999. On the pavements we can follow aspects of the history of Doncaster and the world portrayed on beautiful hand-made bricks and tiles. The Time Line owes much to the artistic abilities of Brian Jackson and Lesley Fallais but would not have been possible without the involvement of many local children and adults. This part of the project will serve as an example for town street schemes in other areas. *(Neil Firth/DMBC)*

The pedestrianised area along French Gate, Christmas 1997. Even allowing for the winter gloom, the street furniture and token plantings in the central area present a very dull scene. *(Neil Firth/DMBC)*

A much happier urban environment in French Gate, with its unique Town Map feature as part of the Quality Streets treatment, during 1999. The stainless steel fencing and seating is by David Mayne; the topiary sculptures in bronze and etched granite are by David Mayne and Victoria Brailsford, who also created the sculptures from Cumbrian sandstone; while Jan Harley and Lyndale Fozard, with the help of local people, created the performance area here, using hand-made bricks and terrazzo. *(Eddie Dixon)*

Most of the buildings along Priory Place have interesting façades, especially above eye-level, but the street itself is purely functional as can be seen in this excellent view dating from about 1996. *(Eddie Dixon)*

After improvements during 1997, Priory Place now has a street surface, wide pavements and elegant lighting that complements rather than competes with adjacent buildings and it is much pleasanter to walk along even though it is still used by traffic. *(Neil Firth)*

Modern buildings don't have to be eyesores. Yates's Wine Lodge is a new and handsome brick building with Georgian-style windows, traditional ground-floor arches and a distinctive corner tower. Its appearance adds interest to Cleveland Street and is a result of the positive partnership between its private owners and the Council's Planning Department. (*Author*)

Priory Walk, linking Printing Office Street to High Street, is an attractive new private development which has involved a great deal of consultation with Doncaster MBC. It was a strange sight to see the Australian-style Walkabout bar packed full of football supporters for England's World Cup matches. Priory Walk was the location chosen for the launch of the *Doncaster Renaissance Town Charter 2002*. The event was discussed in some detail under the heading 'A Town we can be Proud of?' in the *Doncaster Free Press* of 20 June 2002, the Charter being referred to as 'the Town Team's Utopian vision for the development of Doncaster over the next 25 years'. A concluding statement in the Charter refers to the Council's admirable commitment to the 'involvement and participation of its citizens in formulating public policy'. (*Author*)

A great deal of engineering work has been carried out over the last couple of years in improving the appearance of the town centre when approached from the north-east along Church Way. This footbridge, for example, had been placed in a position that almost totally obscured the view of the magnificent architecture of St George's Church. *(Neil Firth)*

Probably the biggest eyesore and blight on the townscape was the multi-storey car park, thankfully demolished during the creation of the new St George's roundabout and bridge. *(Neil Firth)*

St George's Church in all its splendour can now be appreciated from a number of viewpoints, as shown by this example, taken from the ground-level car park. *(Author)*

Part of the attractive new waterfront area and St George's Bridge, 16 June 2002. (*Author*)

New buildings can complement older neighbouring structures when they combine traditional elements with modern materials and an interesting design. The outstanding feature of St Peter in Chains Church is its octagonal form – a pleasing and impressive sight when viewed from Chequer Road. The foundation stone here was blessed and laid in June 1972 by the Right Revd Gordon Walker, Bishop of Leeds. (*Author*)

The restored late seventeenth-century dovecote and attached farm building at West End, Sykehouse. This listed building is now both a dwelling and an office, and yet its historic external and internal features have been retained. (*Author*)

A tremendous amount of work has been carried out in recent years in restoring the gardens at Brodsworth Hall, described by the architectural historian Marc Girouard as 'the most complete surviving example of a Victorian country house in England'. Head gardener David Avery is sitting in front of the fountain which may now be restored to life subject to funding from a lottery grant. *(Doncaster Free Press/South Yorkshire Newspapers)*

In the early hours of Monday 17 January 1994 a fire started in the Market Hall adjoining the Corn Exchange, a Grade II* listed building within the Market Place Conservation Area, resulting in the destruction of its fine Victorian glass and timber roof. A huge restoration project gave the opportunity for archaeological excavations on a site once occupied by the medieval church and churchyard of St Mary Magdalene. One trench revealed five human skeletons. The remains have been left in situ, protected by a layer of sand and a specially cast concrete slab. Restoration also allowed the construction of an imaginative new floor level – the Forum – linked to The Gallery by staircases. This area now caters for a variety of exhibitions, entertainment and community activities. While having a cup of tea in the tea room visitors can read about the history of the market and the town through a series of colourful display panels. Renovating the old market place will be of great importance to the renaissance of the town centre. *(DMBC)*

An aerial view of the Tuby Funfair at Waterdale in the late 1990s. This area of Doncaster has been earmarked for extensive regeneration as an arts, educational and cultural quarter. According to the *Doncaster Renaissance Town Charter 2002*, the quality of existing buildings such as the Central Library and College will be enhanced and complemented by new structures. Another feature will be the creation of a high-quality public space, so it is hoped that traditional events such as funfairs will continue. *(Roger Tuby Archive)*

An artist's impression of Doncaster's proposed New Performance Venue at the Waterdale. *(Glen Howells)*

Acknowledgements

M y thanks go to all the local commercial photographers and postcard publishers of the early decades of the twentieth century who helped to record so many street scenes, people and events. Two, three or more generations after they were active, their surviving work continues to be appreciated by anyone interested in Doncaster and the surrounding areas. Where known, a credit is shown at the end of relevant caption.

I would like to express my sincere thanks to the following people and organisations for assistance with photographic and other material: Brian Barber, Malcolm Billingham, Richard Buckley, Peter Catt, Bernie and Anita Chapman, Doncaster Belles Ladies Football Club, *Doncaster Free Press* (South Yorkshire Newspapers), Doncaster Metropolitan Borough Council (especially staff from the Local Studies and Reference Libraries; Planning & Engineering Departments at Danum House and Scarbrough House; Leisure & Amenities; Inhouse Graphics; Tourist Information; and staff at the Office of the Mayor), Angela Elliott, Hannah Elliott, Norman Ellis, Kath Finlay, Neil Firth, Stanley Frith, Harvester Archers Archery Club, Eric Hepworth, Geoffrey Howse, Norman and Doris Kitching, Peter Lamb, Derek and Marion Mould, Alan and Valerie Paley, Edwin Pretty, Aiden Rave, David Scott, Chris Sharp, Martin Sill, Beckie Swift, Mike Tomlinson, Roger Tuby and family, Mary Wilkinson and Martin Winter (Mayor of Doncaster).

Doncaster Lakeside is one of the Borough's flagship regeneration projects. This could develop into a huge leisure, business and residential area, even larger than Euro-Disney. A 52-acre man-made lake will form the centrepiece of the development, with a marina and water sports facilities. New users of the area include Warner Brothers, Asda, BT, P&O, Portola, Ventura and Green Flag, and the area will extend to the Yorkshire Outlet. *(Eddie Dixon/DMBC)*